NEVER ENOUGH
THE CREATIVE LIFE OF ALEX JORDAN

OTHER BOOKS BY THE AUTHOR

A Mythic Obsession: The World of Dr. Evermor

NEVER ENOUGH
THE CREATIVE LIFE OF ALEX JORDAN

by Tom Kupsh

WINDY CITY PUBLISHERS
CHICAGO

NEVER ENOUGH
THE CREATIVE LIFE OF ALEX JORDAN

Windy City Publishers
2118 Plum Grove Road, #349
Rolling Meadows, IL 60008
www.windycitypublishers.com

Published in the United States of America

First Edition: 2014

ISBN:
978-1-935766-96-4

Library of Congress Control Number:
2014933369

For all who labor backstage

Acknowledgements

I want to thank Art and Karen Donaldson, the owners of The House on the Rock, for their support of this book and their continued commitment to preservation and promotion of the work of Alex Jordan. Thanks to Sue Donaldson, president of The House on the Rock, for her help and access to the archives and photographs used in this book.

A special thanks to Doug Moe, whose 1990 biography of Alex Jordan provided a framework for organization of this book. Doug's written transcripts of the interviews he conducted at that time were of great value to me.

Thanks to my wife Lisa Anne for her patient work as my first reader, first editor, and critic. Thanks to Charlotte Kupsh for her work as my second reader and editor. Thanks to Becky Craig for her help with the photographs.

Table of Contents

Please Read This

Alex Jordan liked to tell the story of an English Lord who had stipulated in his will that his remains should be mummified and kept standing in a glass case in the library of his estate. The Lord further directed that in the minutes of estate board meetings held in the room he should be noted as "Present but not voting." Walking through the corridors and buildings of the vast complex of The House on the Rock, nobody can doubt that Alex Jordan is present. Thousands visit each year and marvel and are puzzled at his creations; most leave with head-shaking questions about who this was and what the place is all about. Much has been written over the years, but nothing has plumbed his creative process or given direction to thoughts about the meaning of his work or its place in American culture. This book is about that creativity and the place of his work in the larger world.

Alex Jordan lived his life in compartments. Ask twelve people who knew him and they would paint a portrait of twelve characters, all incomplete portrayals, incomplete, but accurate; if they joined him at any point along the arc of his life, the twelve might create yet different portraits. It has been nearly twenty-five years since Alex's death and many of the primary sources of information have passed away. The observations and claims of some other witnesses have not withstood the test of time, so the biographer's job is a process of culling out unreliable accounts and finding the reasonable story line that joins the events together. The passage of time, which has deprived us of voices of the past, is nonetheless helpful in gaining a perspective on events. For some, it was a process of healing the wounds of the past and gaining the ability to look back dispassionately and even with a sense of humor.

This biography has as its central emphasis the creative life of Alex Jordan. Everything serves this central theme; information about Alex's business dealings, his personal life, and the personalities around him are treated according to the contribution they made to his creative life.

Who am I to write this? I came to work for Alex Jordan in 1977 as a sculptor and spent over six years of intensive work with him, during an extremely creative period in his life. We developed a good working relationship and he shared his plans and ideas for the future with me through conversations we had while he sat, sometimes for hours, and I worked. The conversations should not be misconstrued as deep discussions. It was more like this: if I sensed that he was not in a bad mood, I might ask a question about his designs and he would give short answers and sometimes he would launch into a full blown detailed description. Once in a while he would bring in his notebooks and go over his sketches of future projects with me, explaining them in detail, or in a sort of design shorthand that we both understood. In addition we shared each other's books and magazines. The workshops were sometimes where he held court. A small parade of collectors, dealers, and contractors passed through trying to sell him something, or were invited in to be amazed by the chaos and extreme hoarding in the workshops and storage areas. I learned very little of the past from all this—he was never interested in the past and if asked he would shrug his shoulders and say, "I don't know." What I did learn was his intent and the design language of Alex Jordan and The House on the Rock.

I left his employment in early 1984. In the summer of 1989 he called me in Seattle and asked me to come back to help him out; I returned shortly before his death later that year. From then until 1998 I served as creative director of The House on the Rock and it was during this period that I learned more about Alex's history and the history of The House on the Rock through the stories circulating among those who had worked with him. I also gained a more thorough knowledge of the buildings and exhibits. In my mind I began a process, almost unconsciously at first, of sifting and winnowing—separating the chaff from the wheat. I was trying to find out what was myth, what was a lie, and what was left.

I left The House on the Rock in 1998 and was again asked to return in 2006 by Art Donaldson, who had purchased the attraction from Alex in 1988. This time I had the title of creative consultant and in this capacity I designed the first extensive remodel of the attraction in fifty years. As part of the job,

I managed the storage of the archives. Alex saved everything. For example, The House on the Rock has torn tickets from forty years ago, every letter asking for information from the 1960s through the 1980s, invoices for window replacements Alex's father ordered in the 1950s, etc. Also housed in the archives is a photographic record of The House on the Rock from the beginning, Alex's family photos going back generations, and all of the business records, including records of acquisitions spanning Alex's entire history at The House on the Rock. Nearly every newspaper and magazine article published about the attraction is also archived. His drawings and notebooks were of special interest to me as I then reviewed at leisure the drawings and notes he had shown me thirty years before, and also looked at the ideas and plans he had not shown me.

I was fortunate to have my first book, *A Mythic Obsession*, published in 2008. It is the biography of Tom Every, a visionary artist who worked with Alex in the 1970s. It was shortly after the successful publication of that book and its positive reception among those who know Tom, that I thought seriously about writing the biography of Alex Jordan. The authorized biography, *Alex Jordan: Architect of his Own Dream*, by Doug Moe was written in 1990, shortly after Alex's death and has sold thousands of copies since. I owe a large debt of gratitude to Doug for his solid work, without which this new book would have been very much harder to attempt. I also made use of Doug's hand-written transcripts and notes from the interviews he conducted at the time.

That's who I am to write Alex Jordan's biography. In the interest of full disclosure, the reader needs to know the following two facts:

First, throughout my time with Alex Jordan I, like all of those who were successful in working for him, always kept my eyes open for tell-tail signs of his moods. A harsh word never passed between us during those years. I came to know the signs that the volcano was about to erupt; I had seen him turn a jaundiced eye on a few people as he made up his mind and their time was over. I visited Alex in his hospital room shortly before he died in November 1989 and saw that eye turned on me. His good opinion, for reasons then unknown to me, had been lost forever. I was saddened, but did not judge the value of our relationship based on the judgment of a dying man. Rather, I kept in mind the years of good relations that we had had.

Second, I am at the time of this writing, employed by The House on the Rock as a creative consultant. This book was not written at the direction or under the sponsorship of the owners of The House on the Rock or anyone else. It is a private enterprise done with my own resources and presented for publication on my own.

While I was writing this biography, I kept in mind two things: usually, the truth stands somewhere in the middle, between the extremes. And, I remembered what Walt Whitman mused, reflecting that somebody would one day write his biography:

"…And so will someone when I am dead and gone write my life?
(as if any man really knew aught of my life,
Why even I myself I often think know little or nothing of my real life,
Only a few hints, a few defused faint clews [sic] and indirections
I seek for my own use to trace out here)."

Tom Kupsh
Spring Green, Wisconsin
March 3, 2014

CHAPTER 1

"SEND THESE, THE HOMELESS, TEMPEST-TOST [SIC] TO ME I LIFT MY LAMP BESIDE THE GOLDEN DOOR!"[1]

Crossing the Atlantic in the middle of the nineteenth century was an act of faith, or maybe an act of ignorance. Few immigrants understood exactly what they were in for. Maybe it was an act of hope, more than anything else, that made them put out of their minds the dangers of the passage. Some sailed for love, or the hope of love, or something like that. They came in families, they came with friends from the same village, and some came alone, a few things packed in trunks—all for a new beginning.

She came alone from Schaffhausen in northern Switzerland and we will never know what mix of hope and love she carried with her. We can have our suspicions because she told her story again and again throughout her life, and not without seasoning it with a little bitterness. Her name was Maria Dorothea Schachenmann, she was twenty-three years old and worked as a hostess in the Raben Haus in Schaffhausen, an establishment owned by the Seiler family. Maria's family operated a large winery in Schaffhausen. The Seilers and Maria's parents agreed to a marriage to Alexander Seiler (III) but the young people were not interested. Maria had her eye on a young man from the village but after much urging from both sides the couple gave in and the arrangements went forward.[2]

The Seiler family left for America in 1848 and planned to have Maria join them after they were established in the New World. It is not quite clear why they decided to leave Switzerland but descendants speculated that it was to get away for the unrest and civil wars raging at the time. The Seiler family had a long history of involvement in politics; there is some suspicion that they may have ended up on the wrong side of the government, and were ostracized from political activities. The only member of the Seiler family remaining behind was grandfather Alexander (I) who at age seventy-seven was judged too frail to travel. They were right—the old man died not long after his family left. In Schaffhausen, they thought he had passed away not so much from ill health as from loneliness.

During the next year, after the Seilers left for America, Maria's family began to prepare her for departure; friends and relatives filled trunks and boxes with her wedding trousseau of "fine things" and gifts for her new life in America. The time came and she left all that was familiar and made her way to the coast, probably traveling down the nearby Rhine to The Netherlands where she boarded a ship for America.

The Atlantic was in no mood to make this easy. In the middle of the forty-nine-day voyage the ship was engulfed in a fierce storm. Fearing for the loss of their lives, the captain and crew needed to lighten the ship so they began throwing cargo overboard including the passengers' trunks. Maria could do nothing but watch as the crew cast her trunks, one after another, into the sea. When she had only one trunk left, Maria had had enough. She sat down on the trunk, spread her skirts out over it, and set her jaw—the crew did not bother her.

When she landed in New York there was still a difficult journey ahead. Travel to the interior of the country (to Wisconsin) in 1849 was difficult; there were few reliable roads and the railroads were in their infancy. The best way to travel was by water. Many immigrants sailed up the Hudson River to Albany where they boarded horse-drawn packet boats traveling the 360 miles to Buffalo and Lake Eire at four miles per hour. The travel and accommodations were better than the bone-jarring stagecoaches of the day, but still rough and cramped. From Albany she boarded a ship for the West. Maria arrived in Milwaukee, which was by then a boom own of 10,000, where she would have heard the familiar sounds of the German language. Milwaukee was beginning to take on a German flavor by then, as people just like Maria fled their homeland and came to America and the Midwest for a better life. There she boarded a stagecoach with her trunk and her hopes for the rough trip some hundred miles west through the wilderness to the Seiler homestead.

And then the rains began—not light misty rains, but stormy downpours soaking everything and making the roads a mire of mud. The storms continued and by the time she arrived in Madison it had been thirty days since she had landed in New York. Madison in 1849 was a frontier town; there was only one identifiable thoroughfare, King Street, and it was rutted and still filled with stumps from the recent clearing of the land. The Wisconsin wilderness began at the edge of the village. In Madison she hired a man with a team and a wagon for the twenty-five-mile trip north to Roxbury and the Seiler place. The driver knew where she was headed and went off his regular route to take her to the homestead. It had been three months since she had left her home in Switzerland. In those days mail service was slow, or non-existent, and the Seiler family had no idea that Maria was coming.

The wagon stopped, the driver lifted down her trunk and she got out in the rain, her shoes settling into the mud. And there she was, Maria and her trunk, in the mud. She looked down at her muddy skirts and at her trunk. Then she looked at the Seiler place there was nothing there, nothing but stumps, the mud, and a rough tent shelter some way off. She turned and looked at the wagon disappearing into the distance, hurrying to make up for lost time, then she looked back at the homestead.

The Seilers came out. They were muddy, the men bearded and rough looking. They did not look like the gentle townspeople she had known in Switzerland. The family brought Maria to their crude shelter, really just a tent. Mrs. Seiler (Caroline) and her two daughters welcomed and comforted her but it took a long time for her to adjust to the rough realities of pioneer life in the Wisconsin of the mid-1800s; it was very different from the life she had known in Schaffhausen. Since the Seiler family had arrived in Wisconsin late in 1848 they had struggled to clear the land and build a house, but the going was hard and slow. Years later Maria would still feel that she had been deceived and carried some resentment with her throughout her life; but for now, here in this muddy tent, she was out of choices.

Within the year the Seilers had built two houses—larger one for the family (five children) and a smaller one for Maria and Alexander (III). The couple were married on December 10, 1849, and settled into their new home. Eventually the children of the elder Seilers married and moved away;

the parents (Alexander II) moved to Madison where they started a house painting business. Maria and Alexander (III) moved into the big house on the farm and by 1856 they had four children: Alexander (IV), Mary, Esther, and Eliza. They were less than happy on the farm; the work was backbreaking and Maria was discouraged by the lack of cultural opportunities, schools, or even a Lutheran church where she could worship.

Maria and her daughters occasionally accompanied friends to services at St. Norbert Catholic Church in Roxbury. The church had been founded by a German priest, Father Adelbert Inama, who built the first log structure on the site himself and immediately began his work of serving the small Catholic community and proselytizing the neighboring Protestants and Native Americans. Maria and her daughters were invited by friends to attend services at St. Norbert parish and eventually converted to Catholicism. They were baptized, in November of 1861 along with Maria's new baby daughter Ida. Her husband Alexander (III), as well as her son, Alexander (IV) remained Lutheran.

Maria and Alexander continued to live on the farm regardless of the fact that they were both unhappy. Alexander found time to lose himself in his passion—botanical studies. He had studied botany at university in Switzerland for a few years and continued his studies on his own in America. During his twenty-nine years of life in America, he would steal away in spare moments to collect specimens and make field drawings of the New World wild flora of southern Wisconsin. He had the reputation of being a skilled artist.

June 17, 1877, was one of those steamy, humid, hot summer days that makes the corn grow and the people wilt. Maria and the girls were at church and Alexander was worshipping in his own way—out in the fields making his botanical drawings, heedless of the heat and humidity. When Maria returned she found him prostrate with sunstroke. Her first thought was to call the priest. Alexander, gravely ill, consented to be baptized into the Catholic faith, received the last rites of the church, slipped into a coma, and passed away. He was fifty-two.

When news of his passing came to the Seiler family in Madison, they were shocked to hear of his conversion and felt that the dying man had been taken advantage of. They arrived with a Protestant minister but Maria and the priest took control of the coffin and the elder Seilers yielded to avoid a conflict. He was not buried in the family plot in Madison as the elder Seilers wished but in the St. Norbert Church cemetery in Roxbury.

Maria's older daughters Eliza and Esther were married before their father's death. In 1871 Mary (Maria and Alexander III's third daughter) married the son of a nearby neighbor Michael Jordan who would become the grandfather of Alex Jordan. Eventually, the remaining Seiler daughter, Ida, grew up, married and moved away, leaving Maria—Alex Jordan's great-grandmother—alone on the farm where she died in May of 1884.

Alexander Seiler III   Maria Seiler

George Pregler, Alex Jordan's maternal grandfather, emigrated from Germany to New York in 1880 where he worked for two years and in 1882 moved to Madison with his wife Magdalena. He was twenty-eight years old. George was an industrious, hard worker with an entrepreneurial spirit. They rented a small cottage at the edge of a swamp in what is today the downtown area of Madison where they were some of the first residents of this low-lying section of the city. By 1893, George and Magdalena had five children, the middle daughter, Magdalena (Lena) born in 1888, would become the mother of Alex Jordan.

George Pregler took a job working nights shoveling coal to serve the two steam trains at the nearby train depot. Soon he saved enough money to buy a milk cow and sold the milk to supplement the family income. Like so many immigrants, he looked for opportunities to better himself; he did not have very much, but where others saw ashes and a swamp, he recognized opportunity. With the profits from his milk sales and night work at the depot he saved $5,000, a sizeable sum in those days. He used the money to buy nineteen acres of the marshland near where he had been renting. This region became know as Pregler's Addition, later it was called Greenbush. In a 1916 interview for *The Wisconsin State Journal* he recalled those early years: "I saw that Greenbush was going to be a paying proposition some day so I and my wife just worked hard and bought it with our savings. When I got it, I figured that it would pay me to build little homes on the filled-in marshland, so during the day, I worked at night, I built them. Most of the people who bought my land and houses are doing well now, as land in the business section here is worth almost as much as it is up town."[3]

He filled in the marsh with ash from the depot and whatever other fill he could find, bought old houses and moved them to the newly created lots and repaired them. From almost the beginning of the settlement, Madison developers had been filling in low spots and even the shallow shoreline of the lakes to create new land. He sold the homes to newly arriving immigrants, many of them poor Italians, for $5 down and $5–$10 per month. Still keeping his night job, he began to build houses of brick and lumber with his own hands, doing all the work himself. The conditions in Greenbush, as in a great deal of Madison, were primitive by today's standards—crowded with no indoor plumbing. In spite of the privations of the times, Greenbush became a thriving ethnic Italian community, although some later referred to it as a ghetto. In 1916 the Greenbush neighborhood was a prosperous community and George Pregler was proud of his contribution to the city of Madison, recalling: "I never foreclosed a single mortgage in all the years that I have been in business in spite of the fact that payments were slow and very small."[4] At the end of the twentieth century former residents looked back upon their time there with a nostalgic eye.

The Pregler Family, Magdalena on right

Conrad and Barbara Jordan came from Germany to New York in the first half of the nineteenth century. Their son Michael Jordan (Alex Jordan's paternal grandfather) was born in New York State in 1840. The lure of rich and cheap land brought Michael to the farmlands of rural Wisconsin seeking a better life. The Jordan farm was near the Seiler homestead and that's where Michael and Mary Seiler met and were married.

Alex Jordan's father, Alexander P. Jordan, was born to Michael and Mary (Seiler) Jordan on the family farm near Roxbury, Wisconsin in 1883, the middle child with four older siblings and four younger. His older brothers Conrad and John grew up and left the farm to start a meat business in Madison, and when Alex came of age he joined them, working in one of the several markets that they owned. In Madison he met George Pregler's daughter Magdalena (Lena). They were married at St. James Church in Madison in 1911. It was a fairly elaborate double wedding ceremony. Lena's older brother George and his bride were married along with Lena and Alex Sr. The newly married couple moved into one of George Pregler's homes in the Greenbush.

Alex Jordan Sr. and Magdalena Pregler

Alex Jordan Sr. and Magdalena Pregler (right) Wedding Photo

Magdalena (Lena) gave birth to their first child, Florence Katharine, in May of 1912. She died before her third birthday. Alexander John Jordan Jr. was born on March 3, 1914.

Alex Jordan Jr.

Alex was by all accounts a happy, healthy boy. Lena made sure that Junior was given a Catholic education at St. James School under the guidance of the sisters of Notre Dame. Alex, by Lena's own admission, was something of a spoiled child and always got his way; he needed all the guidance he could get and frequently clashed with the nuns. Alex's parents were strong, hard working, and thrifty; they expected Junior to follow their lead.

Lena was deeply religious, not a sentiment shared by her husband or later by Junior. The family moved to several homes in Madison ending up in University Heights where Alex attended Holy Redeemer Elementary School. There he received his primary education intertwined with the doctrines of the Catholic Faith.

The Jordan family at home

CHAPTER 2

THE EARLY YEARS OF ALEX JORDAN

As the 1920s began, Alex Sr. followed the example of his father-in-law George Pregler, left the meat business, and began to pursue his fortunes in real estate. Some early success in the roaring twenties real estate market prompted him to expand. He hired noted architect Frank Riley to design a residence for single female university students, they called the building The Villa Maria.

Frank Riley was by then a well-known architect who had earned his degree from MIT and was much influenced by his travels in Great Britain, Italy, and Germany. The buildings he designed after World War I in Madison show Riley rooted in European tradition and a promoter of the Colonial Revival. Among his buildings are The Governor's Mansion, The Madison Club, Madison East High School, and The Villa Maria, all of which are conservative, even retro designs. In fact, the Villa Maria seems to be incongruous, as if it had been uprooted from the Mediterranean coast and plopped down near the shores of Lake Mendota, but it was what the Jordans wanted.

Riley was the polar opposite of another architect working in and around Madison at the time, the innovative Frank Lloyd Wright, who was much less successful than Riley in selling his designs in post-war Madison.

The Villa Maria

Alex Jordan Sr., for all his reputed strictness, may have been something of a dreamer and perhaps overreached; it was not easy from the very beginning. The $60,000 bank loan and other dealings found the Jordans in constant debt for years to come, owing sizeable interest payments to banks, vendors, and family while the country was on the eve of the Depression. They were tough minded, hard working, and frugal; John Mitby, long-time attorney for Alex Jr., remarked, "Alex [Jr.] didn't have it easy early in his life. He had to figure out a way to survive. He didn't have much. People have suggested he had [money] all his life. This was a very poor man for a long, long period of time."⁵ Junior was expected to do his share of the work and, as he became able, help with improvements and repairs on the Villa. The foundations of a frugal builder, a tough dreamer who understood business and hard work were being laid in Junior even if he resisted at the time.

In 1928 after his completion of elementary school, Alex was enrolled in St. Norbert's High School, a Catholic boarding school connected with St. Norbert's College in DePere, Wisconsin. One suspects Lena sent him to St. Norbert's to ensure the continuation of his Catholic training and to keep him on the straight and narrow. Fat chance—he would soon wander away from any religion, but the liberal education provided at St. Norbert's gave Alex a firm foundation in the canon of English literature which would provide him with inspiration and pleasure his whole life as well as a knowledge of the sweep of western European history which added to his understanding of the world around him. He came away from his secondary education with an inborn curiosity, inventiveness, a voracious appetite for everything, and he was well prepared to learn.

He was well on his way to his adult six feet two inches and 200-plus pounds when he played fullback for the high school team in the era of leather-helmet, head-down, straight-ahead, cloud-of-dust, everybody-gets-a-black-eye, football. He was also a youthful amateur boxer; nobody can doubt that there was a side of his life that was pugilistic. He earned a reputation as a clever prankster and showed skill with his hands, building ship models and experimenting with electronic devices. A 1987 story related in *Knight Life*, St. Norbert's school magazine, gives some insight into the young Alex.[6] The story is related by one of his high school classmates and describes a card trick he and Alex played on younger students. Alex stared into their eyes and claimed he could read their minds and always identified the correct card they picked from the deck. His mind reading was helped by a cohort who peeped through a hole from the attic above and signaled Alex using an electronic device that Alex fashioned. The magazine went on to describe Alex as "a boy full of fun and life with a high sense of adventure, creativity, and a knowledge and love of electronic gadgets." This early view of Alex gives hints of some of his core characteristics easily identified in his work thirty years on—Alex Jordan the trickster, illusionist, and showman who shape changed and dazzled from behind the curtain and left everyone wondering. His pranks were now of a harmless variety, but that would not always be the case.

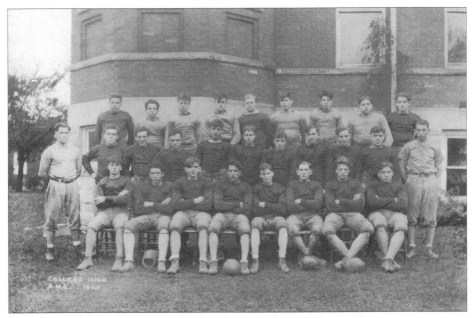

St. Norbert 1930 Football Team, Alex, back row—fourth from right

After graduation in 1932 he made several starts at college but he really wasn't interested. Alex was unsure about what he wanted to do and began drifting from one thing to another, searching for a creative outlet for his boundless energy.

High School graduation photo

The 1920s and 1930s were difficult for the family and Junior was now expected to do a greater share of the maintenance and construction work at Villa Maria. It was soon evident that Alex was growing into a strong young man with extraordinarily skilled hands. Alex worked at a variety of jobs as a young man; later he called these his butterfly years. Work was not easy to find in the Depression: he drove a cab, worked in a battery factory, and continued to work for his father remodeling and repairing Villa Maria where he learned some of the basic carpentry skills that would serve him well in the future. All the while he continued to cultivate a broad range of interests.

Alex was always designing or building something. He came up with the idea of creating a custom car using the body and running gear from an early 1930s Cadillac V16 roadster. He did the planning and Harry Whitehorse, whose family ran an auto body shop, did the welding. They left the Cadillac pretty much the way it was, just adding custom body parts—fenders, a hood, etc. He drove around town creating a scene wherever he went, at times sporting a rubber nose, and with a cigar in hand he wowed the crowds with stories about getting the car from movie star Ann Sheridan. He intimated years later that the car served him well as something of a chick magnet. Twenty years later spotting a picture of the car on the wall of the workshop, he walked over to it, starred a long time, and mused, "What a car!" The car ended up being sold in the 1950s and met its end in a junkyard near Janesville where Alex's friend Tom Every found it thirty years later with small trees growing up through it. When Tom asked Alex if he wanted to buy it, Jordan said, "No, we can build a better one." It was decision he later regretted.[7]

The Custom Car

He was living life in the fast lane screaming around town in his custom car. Alex was out for excitement and trouble and he found both. He became a heavy drinker and smoked up to four packs of cigarettes a day, admitting some years later that, "If I got down to two packs left, I'd get in a panic and have to run out and get more." He took everything to extremes and was interested in anything that was fast and exciting, skidding across the frozen lake in an iceboat and later learning to fly. He was pushing himself and everyone around him to the limit.

Jennie Olson grew up on a farm in southwestern Wisconsin; the work was hard and unrelenting. Her father was an authoritarian man who thought that girls did not need to go past the fifth or sixth grade because after that they would just be looking for a man or getting pregnant. The one thing Jennie knew was that she wanted to get away from the farm. As soon as she could, she moved to Madison where she got a job in a laundry and later as a clerk in a drug store.

If young people in Madison wanted to have a great time in the late 1930s they could board a ferry and cross the lake to a dancehall outside the city limits. During prohibition, dancehalls that regularly hosted big bands found they could do business better if they were located away from troublesome authorities. By then prohibition was only an unpleasant memory but the dancehalls, many on the outskirts of town, continued to be popular attractions. Jennie Olson had a date that night and they danced to the big band music until a "big and handsome man" cut in, took her in his arms and it was an enchanted evening. She fell in love with Alex immediately. They would be together in one way or another for the next fifty years.[8]

Jennie Olson, 1930s

They began to spend time together. Alex always saw people fishing on the lake and wondered what that was all about so he got a boat and fishing tackle and took Jennie out on the lake. They fished for a while and nothing happened so he took all the fishing gear and threw it over the side and went back to shore—that was the end of fishing.[9]

In the rocky years that were to come Jennie was for him a commonsense anchor to reality, down-to-earth and practical in contrast with his creative flights. She never put herself forward but was always there in the background as his constant companion and refuge. She saw her share of his fits of anger but she also saw the triumph of his creativity and quietly shared in that success. One of her fondest memories related after his passing was the day she was frightened out of her wits and thrilled at the same time, hanging on for dear life as they careened across the lake in his ice boat, his thin coat flapping in the wind.[10] We can only speculate about their life together because they were both private people and were reticent to talk about personal things. At this writing no one was available to shed more light on their relationship. But it is hard to get past that image of the iceboat—maybe it is an awful lot like their life together.

After his mother's death in 1969 he asked Jennie to move in to the family home with him. Her response was, "I don't want to be your mother." She understood that Lena, who never liked her, had been the one who ruled that roost and the one who took care of Alex, mothering him to the end. Alex assured her that it wouldn't be that way and she consented and moved in.

There are scant reliable stories and her occasional reminiscences to friends and family after his death. The common threads paint a picture of an intimate relationship between the two of them growing older and closer; by all accounts she adored him. When she needed to have her pacemaker replaced in the late 1970s Alex was worried. He reflected, "If something happens to her, you'll see one guy fade pretty fast." All agree she was a very proper lady, thoughtful and kind; perhaps in the end, in spite of her warnings, she mothered Alex.

For his part, he found their home a refuge from his work where he could relax with just the two of them there. Alex told Julie Esser, who functioned as their personal assistant at the end of his life, that Jennie and he had a good relationship because he could forget about The House on the Rock and talk about it when he wanted to.[11] There are no pictures of the two of them together—the speculation is that there never was anyone else there to take a picture. He loved animals and taught their little dogs to do tricks and doted on them. She baked cookies and always remembered to send cards on everyone's birthday. This is who they were and how they were after 1969. For the rest—we only have a few hints.

In 1981 Edna Meudt, well-known Wisconsin regional poet and editor of the short-lived *Uplands Reader*, interviewed Alex Jordan in the Carousel Room at The House on the Rock. They had known each other for years and Edna was something of an admirer of Alex. During their talk, Edna presented him with a photograph taken by her friend Edgar Obma: the photograph showed the dark brooding figure of Alex Jordan in front of his canted windows and was inscribed "Citizen Kane." They both laughed.

Then Alex talked about how Hearst is only remembered for his "yellow journalism" and not for his philanthropic work. And then she writes, "I began a quotation: 'The evil men do lives after them,' then stopped, certain that no one was listening. Alex Jordan picked it up: 'The good is oft' interred with their bones; so let it be with Caesar.' The weary lines in his face lifted, a smile made brilliant his blue eyes."[12] "The evil men do," certainly describes the dark and shameful events that occurred in 1939 which scandalized his family, served as a sword for his detractors, and it did live after him.

Alex and his friend Sid Boyum experimented with photography. Sid took photography seriously, for Alex it was just another passing interest. The two of them teamed up for one money-making scheme after another: selling Portland cement as a repair glue for nylon stockings, marketing cheese to students, and using Sid's photographic expertise, taking infrared photos of people's houses and trying to sell them to homeowners. And it was with a camera that Alex went down a dark path.

Alex Jordan carried within him a dark daemon; when it emerged, all rules, decency, friendship, conscience disappeared. In 1939, he was a young man of high energy burning with the restless fires of creativity. He had not yet decided whether he would use this energy for good or ill.

It's called a badger game and it is a con that had been around for a hundred years by the time Alex came up with his version. It is an extortion scheme, usually used on married men, in which the subject is lured into a sexually compromising position and then blackmailed. The victim was a local businessman (Sid Boyum's employer) and the plan was to extort $300 or an offer of employment for Alex. Jennie lured the "mark" into her apartment where Alex was hidden in a closet, camera ready. When the compromising photos were developed, Alex presented them to the victim and made his demands. It was double jeopardy for the victim—give in to blackmail or go to the police and lose his reputation and marriage, and be charged with what was then a crime. He went to the police and Alex and Jennie were arrested, jailed, and pled guilty to misdemeanor extortion; they both got off with a fine. Sid Boyum was questioned by police but was never charged. The Madison newspapers were all but silent.

It is a long way from the picture of Lena's little alter boy Alex in his surplice and cassock to a police mug shot. Alex Jordan Jr. had to decide what he was going to do with his creativity and energy—his decisions so far had not been very good. This event followed Alex all his life and was common, whispered knowledge among The House on the Rock employees. Late in his life it was openly and widely publicized. This crime, low down as it was, tells us something about who Alex was in 1939 and gave easy ammunition to his detractors and those who would demean his accomplishments. Some critics were quick to fall into what in journalism is referred to as the genetic fallacy—pointing to a dark and shameful part of the past and making universal judgments about the present. The facts of these events are clear, but to view Alex only through this dirty lens is to present a distorted picture of this complex character. Alex Jordan was a mixture of extremes and when he was bad, he was bad. This may have been a turning point, for while he was no saint and he carried with him the burden of his faults, he never found himself on the wrong side of the law again. Finally the trickster had been caught and straightened out—to some degree. As for Jennie, it seems that she loved him too much—beyond all reason, and would do anything for him. This shameful lapse was completely out of character with the rest of her life.

In 1942 Alex was rejected for military service because of a heart condition; he worked instead in a national defense job as a steamfitter at Badger Ordnance in Baraboo. He was filled with energy and creativity but still could not settle on a direction for his life. In 1942 his father made him manager of Villa Maria. Alex Sr. sold the Villa Maria in 1945 and put all his efforts toward his construction company, hiring Alex Jr. to help him. Alex continued to be a worry to his parents—he seemed to be wandering aimlessly. He was over thirty years old and still living at home when not at his girlfriend's apartment, he never had a steady job for any length of time, and he had no clear path for the future. He had shamed himself and his parents with his various behaviors and, much to Lena's sorrow, had abandoned religious faith. But the elements of success were within him. On both sides of his family were examples of hard work and an entrepreneurial spirit and his parents were living models of economy and industry. Alex's natural curiosity led him to be interested in everything and to explore everything, reading, listening and taking it all in. And he was constantly tinkering and working with his hands. He returned often to his favorite place, Deershelter Rock in the woods among the hills of southwestern Wisconsin, and it was there that he found the direction for his life.

Alex Jordan, 1930s

CHAPTER 3

"WHEREVER NATURE LED: MORE LIKE A MAN FLYING FROM SOMETHING THAT HE DREADS, THAN ONE WHO SOUGHT THE THING HE LOVED. FOR NATURE THEN (THE COARSER PLEASURES OF MY BOYISH DAYS, AND THEIR GLAD ANIMAL MOVEMENTS ALL GONE BY) TO ME WAS ALL IN ALL...."[13]

Deershelter Rock is in the driftless area of Wisconsin. The state is usually associated with gently rolling hills, fields and flat woodlands, but southwestern Wisconsin is a different terrain entirely. The last age of the glaciers never touched this area, so rather than the smooth landscape of the rest of the state, here winding streams run deep in the valleys, and ancient rock outcroppings stand as landmarks. Oral tradition is that native peoples used the undercut sides of the rock formation known as Deershelter for occasional protection and to this day deer find it a refuge from the wind and cold. The driftless region is the habitat for deer, fox, coyote, and less commonly, black bear and mountain lions. Hawks, eagles, vultures, and a variety of raptors and songbirds fill the evergreen and deciduous trees, pine snakes and rattlers find a home here and the streams bubble with trout. The Wisconsin River makes its broad way lazily through the heart of the region and looks much the same as it did to the French explorers more than 400 years ago. It is a unique topography and natives as well as returning residents talk about a deep and profound connection to this landscape.

Deershelter Rock stands five miles south of the Wisconsin River along State Highway 23, seven miles north of Dodgeville. The sandstone formation rises from the valley floor some 75 feet and the irregular table top stretches more than 200 feet north to south and about 60–75 feet east to west. Observation

Rock is a chimney-rock formation that stands 20 feet out from the northern end of the rock; still further to the north stands Percussion Rock, a massive narrow formation reaching to about the same height as Deershelter. The oral tradition is that the Jordan family picnicked on Deershelter, as did many of the local residents. The rock was a favored spot for outings for a long time before the Jordans arrived. The curiosity is that it was not public land but people seemed to come and go and visit it at their leisure without considering the modern idea of trespassing. It was a time when locals thought nothing of hiking through private land and landowners were mostly tolerant. Certainly the Christiansons, who owned Deershelter Rock and the surrounding 200-plus acres, fell into this category. The Christianson family homesteaded the farm in the 1800s, cleared the land, and built the house and farm buildings.

Picnickers at Deershelter Rock, early 1900s

At first it was just a spot to picnic and party with friends, "a little steak, a small habacci, a whole gallon of Tom Collins." It was just after World War II that Alex first pitched a tent on the rock but high winds ended this venture and then he built what he called a "tarpaper shack" there. He squatted on the rock for quite a while before he made a formal agreement with the landowners, Oscar and Geraldine Christianson, who knew that he was building up there, but did not think much about it. In June 1953 Alex and the Christiansons signed an agreement recognizing that Alex had already built a "cottage" on Deershelter Rock and further granting him a forty-year lease including Deershelter Rock and 100 feet around the base extending in all directions for $7.50 per year. Alex paid for the entire forty years on the spot.

Alex at Deershelter Rock, 1940s

The design of the House has often been compared with Frank Lloyd Wright's work and some people mistakenly think that it was designed by the famous architect. In the 1920s and 1930s, when Alex was growing up in Madison, the architecture of Wright was in evidence. One of the homes that the Jordan family lived in when Alex was a boy was near an early Wright house and Alex would have seen it daily as a child. Some details in The House on the Rock seem to be reminders of the prairie style identified with Wright, for example the low ceilings or the use of native limestone and natural materials. But clearly, nobody would mistake Alex's work for that of Frank Lloyd Wright. Alex's tendencies were not toward the cool, measured, cerebral designs common to Wright; in his work at Deershelter, Jordan built in an impromptu manner using not only his head, but also his guts and more often *cojones*, letting himself be led by nature or happenstance from one thing to another, never worrying about the overall design—one day's work laid the path for the next day's building. Later in his designs for the Gatehouse and the Mill House he took a more studied and planned approach. Alex never saw the interior of Wright's home at Taliesin until The House on the Rock was nearly finished. In a 1976 interview he said, "I deliberately tried to avoid the style of Frank Lloyd Wright, although I am an admirer of his. There's no doubt I was influenced by him...."[14]

Some believe that since The House on the Rock is five miles from Wright's home at Taliesin there is some relationship between the two sites. The spreading of this erroneous idea caused some animosity towards The House on the Rock among members of Wright's Taliesin Fellowship. Alex would have nothing to do with this. Alex Jordan and Frank Lloyd Wright never met, and Alex always spoke respectfully about Mr. Wright. The design and building of The House on the Rock are completely Alex Jordan's. The idea that the origins of The House on the Rock are shrouded in a fit of vengeance against Wright because of a slight to Alex Jordan's father is a widespread apocryphal story worth retelling and examining here. It is a story Alex himself knew his erstwhile friend Sid Boyum had told.

The tale was first told by Sid Boyum in an interview with a *Wisconsin State Journal* newspaper reporter in the late 1980s. The series of articles resulting from this interview and other research were uncomplimentary of Alex's character.[15] Sid had been Alex's youthful comrade and partner in mischief and their tempestuous friendship warmed and cooled through the years. Sid was a gifted illustrator, sculptor, and photographer and a local character on the east side of Madison where he was well known as a teller of tall tales; in fact, Sid was the winner of the Burlington Liars Club World Champion Liar contest in 1976. When he fell out with Alex around 1980 his harmless stories and jokes turned vitriolic toward his old friend. The following is the transcript of an interview conducted in 1990 in which Sid Boyum, who claimed to be a friend of Wright's is telling his story:

> The old man [Alex's father] said he'd like Frank Lloyd Wright's opinion of Villa Maria plans. We went out there... [to Taliesin to speak with Wright]. This is Mr. Jordan from Madison [Boyum said]. He's made some plans for a women's rooming house and I think they're pretty nice. Would you look at them? Wright looked at the plans, he walked around and stood looking out the window [and said], "I wouldn't hire you to design a cheese box for me or a chicken coop." End of interview.

> On route 23 going home, Alex Sr. says, "I'm going to get even with that sonofabitch, I'm going to put a Japanese house up out here." He thought it would irritate Wright so the old man went in there [the farm where Deershelter Rock is] and talked to the farmer. The old man gave him five or ten dollars as a down payment to put that sign up there. And the sign was up there before The House on the Rock was ever built....[16]

The story is filled with errors and inconsistencies. Alex Sr. did not design The Villa Maria; it was designed by well-known Madison architect Frank Riley. Wright would have been familiar with Riley's work, which was all over the city. Sid also claimed that Alex's father worshipped Wright; if this were the case he would have known that Wright would have nothing but contempt for Riley's work and would never have dreamed of showing the Riley plans to the famous architect. The story relates how Sid Boyum introduced Alex Sr. to Wright. In the middle 1920s, when Villa Maria was in the planning stages, Sid would have been a boy of ten (1924)—hardly a friend of Wright's or apt to be making the introduction. Furthermore, the first agreement (an extended lease) with the Christianson family, who owned Deershelter Rock, was made some thirty years later in 1953 and no sign appeared at the road entrance until The House on the Rock opened to the public in 1960.

Whatever Sid Boyum's motivation for this story, it passed away with him in 1991, but the effects of this tale linger on, characterizing the origins of the House as anger at, and parody of, Frank Lloyd Wright—an idea made sad by the falling off of friendship between two old pals. Regardless of all this, Alex spoke of Boyum as "poor Sid" and kept up occasional contact with his old friend, even calling him a few weeks before he (Jordan) died. After Alex passed away, Sid wrote a few rambling letters to the owners of The House on the Rock containing, among other things, unfounded claims of credit for ideas and artifacts at The House on the Rock and asking to be paid for photographs he had taken that Alex used in his publications twenty-five years before. In spite of his bitterness towards Alex Jordan and The House on the Rock, Sid remains an original, humorous, talented artist, and unforgettable character; he should not be underestimated as a sometimes friend and certainly a foil for Alex.[17]

Alex was soon dissatisfied with his tarpaper shack he built on the rock in the late 1940s, tore it down, and began to build something more durable. In his whole creative life he was never afraid to tear down and start over. He was still working for his father repairing apartments and doing some light construction so his project at Deershelter was what he called a "weekender." In the beginning Alex was building a retreat, a hideaway in the country, at first a single room and a place to gather with his friends. He added as he went along and the style of the original house reflects the intention to create a place for conversation, gatherings, and quiet activities like reading or listening to music.

To begin, Alex built a small studio/study near the north end of the rock complete with fireplace and skylight and room for his growing collection of books. The construction materials, including bricks, mortar, lumber and glass all had to be brought up the seventy-five feet up from the valley below. At first he climbed across a fallen tree and scaled the rock. Then, he built a ladder to reach part way up from where he climbed the rock to the top. He carried all the materials on his back, working alone. As he told an interviewer in 1971: "I worked on it for years pretty much alone, didn't have a hoist, carried up the cement, carried up the sand, carried up the water and the timbers. Oh, I was powerful in those days—you wouldn't believe it! Those were the fun years, those first years."[18] He added that he had, "helpers, friends." It turned out that a lot of people thought it was just a great project and were willing to help out.

Later, he made things a little easier when he installed electricity and a power hoist to lift materials up from the valley floor.

Alex working on the House

This Study and the adjoining Living Room made up the beginnings of what would become The House on the Rock, but this simple start was anything but exotic, resembling from the exterior something like a box on a rock. It was his own place, not his father's apartments, and he was beginning to find his own way—he said about the beginnings: "Every kid wants a place of his own, you know, a retreat or something like that."[19]

Early version of the House

The interior of this early version of the living room is rustic and reminiscent of the Colonial style popular at the time; the reproduction furniture is almost suburban. The double fireplace hearth is one of the first of many of ever increasing size he would build. But he was not satisfied, "As soon as I was done [building it] I could see it was all wrong. So I tore it down and started over."[20] More accurately, he tore parts of it down and radically transformed the rest. Never afraid to backtrack, he was fond of repeating, "Only a fool persists in his ignorance, but a wise man can change his mind."

Early version of the Living Room with canted windows

He continued to experiment with the design and developed the cantilevered windows that would soon become a typical feature of the House; since he used no scaffolding, the windows had to be built from the inside out. Alex built these by himself leaning out over the valley tethered to the rock by a rope. He never displayed any fear of heights even as he grew old, walking out on steel beams with nothing below despite the difficult and shuffling gait of his later years. As he developed his designs for the windows they became wider and broader; the effect was to offer a panoramic-treetop view of the valley below and the distant rolling hills. The angle of the windows can also create a dizzying condition in the faint or those prone to vertigo. Later Alex would suggest an even more dramatic effect by building benches against the windows, using the window itself as the backrest.

The Study, with its fireplace, bookshelves, and skylights and small collections, was a comfortable private place to be alone or with one or two people. He kept to himself out here in the middle of nowhere, in what Alex, referring to early American maps called "Indian Country."

The Original Study

In these two early rooms we can begin to trace some themes and tendencies in the creative mind of Alex Jordan. These are the rooms of a hopeless and incurable romantic, furnished with artifacts from the distant past: the flintlock rifle and powder horn, spinning wheel, oil lamps, wolf skin rug, as well as his books, and later, when power came to the House, a shortwave radio and record player. On a shelf at the far end of the room sat his sculptural portrait of Jennie that remains in the House to this day; it was her house too—she helped with construction and mixed mortar for him. She described herself as getting sunburned and as "brown as a bear."[21] But finally she told Alex that the work was too much for her. According to Don Martin, who would soon become Alex's master mason, she was pretty good at it. Over the fireplace he carved verses that catch the spirit of Alex's work here (see end of Chapter).

In the image "The Original Study" we see some clues about what was to come; these are the meager beginnings of his vast collections, ordinary stuff, but in this glassware in the skylights overhead he's not exactly trying to make the viewer below comfortable—discomforting, tilted in, defying gravity (or good sense). This is just Alex playing a little, trying to get us to notice him and the show.

It is an introvert's architecture all about safe interior spaces and privacy and not about exterior design or image—in fact not much related to its surroundings at all. In this early incarnation of The House on the Rock Alex had not yet made his peace with Deershelter Rock—he was working against it. The Study and Living Room are defying the Rock, just attached to it like those windswept Victorian farmhouses of the great plains-treeless, defiant and incongruous.

In 1956 the entire 240-acre Christianson farm became available. Oral tradition tells the story that Alex Jr. built a model of the house he intended to construct on the rock to convince his father of the possibilities of the site.[22] Alex Sr. bought the farm for $12,000 and immediately began investing money in the property. They hired Don Martin as their first full-time employee and Alex and Don, along with occasional helpers, began to plant trees—110,000 in all. Don worked under the direction of Alex Jr. but they were both employees of Alex's father, who held the purse strings. Family businesses can be tough; Alex Sr. paid Don Martin $48 per week at the start while Alex Jr. received $26.50, but he was still living at home and having his mother cook and clean for him. Over the next few years Don's rate of pay rose while Alex's stayed the same. The relationship between father and son had always been complex and uneasy and it would now become more conflicted. As Don Martin put it, "Alex had the ideas and his Dad had the money." Don also speculated that it may have been about the time Alex Sr. bought the land that he started thinking of opening it up to the public, as Don put it, "Why else hire somebody?"[23] Alex's father had by this time gained thirty years of experience in real estate and construction—he was no fool.

Don Martin, Geraldine Christianson's brother, was working on the Christianson farm when Alex leased it. Don recalls the early years: "I didn't know him [Alex] that well then. He leased the rock and I was farming. I wasn't around him much. He liked his privacy." He describes the youthful 250-pound Alex as strong as a bull. In 1957 Alex asked Oscar where he could find some full-time help and Oscar recommended Don and the Jordans hired him. He would continue to work for The House on the Rock through the rest of Alex's life. He recalled the early years: "It was an experience. I guess I was more nervous than anything else. I was nothing but a dumb farmer, a greenhorn. The first year I worked with Alex, I had never laid a stone in my life, or done carpentry work. I had never held a skillsaw in my hand."[24] His lack of knowledge, and Alex's too, led to creative and esoteric solutions to construction problems and ended up enhancing the homemade and personal quality of the construction and design of the House. Don remembers: "Alex didn't really know carpentry. He could lay a stone—he was a very good stonemason. That first year we worked side by side. I guess I was kind of lucky because Alex was never very fussy—if it wasn't square or plumb it didn't matter. If it had, I'd have been fired the first week. He was more interested in the creative effect than in making a building square." Alex reflected on his methods years later saying, "I stay about two days ahead of my workmen. I guess if I should die, this whole thing would end two days later. All the plans are right here." He tapped his head.[25]

Alex now had access to the stone quarry on the farm, a quarry from which Don and Alex would extract tons of limestone to continue to build the House and other structures. Talking about the rock quarry Alex said, "A geologist friend of mine told me the rock is Niagra limestone. It's very hard—with a wedge, you can strike sparks."[26] The geologist also assured Alex that Deershelter Rock, though made of sandstone, would not experience any significant erosion for thousands of years.

In the early years, before the Jordans hired Don Martin, Alex did a great deal of work on the House himself, "I did practically the whole top myself. There was never a master plan—it just developed as I went along. What happens is you start small, build a platform, some place between the rocks…."

As he expanded out on and around the rock he was guided by the profile of the rock, taking what the terrain would give him—he made his peace with where he was. "I did it all—hauled tons of rock, cut holes for the trees. I just bulled my way along." He later reflected, "In the beginning it was all just a pile of rock up here—rocks and trees. We left everything as it was, worked around it, worked with it—that's part of the beauty of the place." He did not destroy any of the rock formations at Deershelter but learned to work in concert with them. Later he also reused lumber from the farm buildings that he and Don tore down, hoisting the barn beams up the face of the rock. From 1956 on his designs became more open and airy. He remodeled and combined the Living Room and the Study, covering the fireplace with limestone from the farm quarry and rebuilding the canted windows in this new open style.

The remodeled Living Room

Among the first rooms he built was the Winter Room with its inglenook fireplace, "I originally wanted to build a room right inside a huge fireplace. It was a good dream, but it didn't work out too well."[27] The Winter Room area did not have enough space to accommodate this dream. He would realize this idea later in the Mill House designs in 1966-68. Between 1956 and 1959, quite gradually the identifiable House on the Rock style took shape. Speaking to a reporter interviewing him in the House in late 1959 he said, "What you see here now has really developed in the last three years." Alex began to collect Asian art and artifacts, kabuki dolls, a brass south Asian brazier later used in the Tea Room, a mother-of-pearl and ivory wedding chest, and other rare collectibles, to enhance the exotic ambience of the House. All of his life he returned to add artifacts to the House and to move things around—it was always a work in progress.

The Winter Room

The House on the Rock style is centered on a series of intimate spaces with low ceilings conducive to conversation in the secure comfort of built-in sofas (dated by their shag carpeting) near heavy fireplaces. The cantilevered windows and alternating interior and exterior spaces in which trees grow in the House and through the House, the boulders in the architecture, the uneven rise and fall of the floors, eventually the sounds of trickling water, the use of natural materials—all this blurred the notion of interior/exterior.

Although he learned a great deal working for his father repairing the family apartments, Alex had only rudimentary carpentry skills when he began to build on Deershelter Rock. He learned as he went along, improving his skills and finding his way. Necessity and inventiveness were his teachers and he did not limit himself to preconceived notions of how things were always done, or what could or could not be built. This attitude of independence and finding his own path was a key element of his creative work—he always stretched the capabilities of the materials and took his structures to the extreme. Added to this was his economy—he built with salvaged materials and only as a last resort bought new. By the time the House was nearly finished he could proudly say, "There's never been a tradesman work here." He had picked up all the trades on the job. Twenty years later when The House on the Rock was fabulously successful, he laughed about himself in those early years saying: "I had this station wagon and I would buy a couple of two-by-fours and put them in the back and bring them out. I only bought a couple because I didn't want to have any left over." His sense of thrift was legendary, as was his desire for solitude.

View through the House from the Dining Room

Once he had broken out of traditional patterns of thinking and definitions of space he began to open the building up in a free flow of space, one "room" flowing into another. He would always refer to the nooks and free-flowing spaces as rooms; some of the spaces are clearly defined as rooms while other areas are rooms in name only.

The area on the rocky surface of Deershelter outside of the few original rooms was at first open space, sometimes bordered by low masonry walls at the edge of the escarpment. He gradually found his way into the grander, and freer spaces, built walls to enclose walkways and patios around the rock, and started to open up his designs, allowing the interior space to flow freely.

Early aerial view of House

Just to the south of the Living Room he closed in the area creating a pergola, one part of which was called the Garden Room and the other the Patio, with lattice work shading the native stone and limestone masonry floor creating a shaded indoor/outdoor space. He tried to plant trees and shrubs but found that, "things don't grow too well. It seems you always have too much shade or too little shade, and too much or too little water."[28] Before long he would install a proper roof over this space, closing it in but leaving a few skylights to let in natural light and holes in the roof for the indigenous trees. Alex never had a green thumb—he was too impatient and thought that because he *said* something should grow there, or would look nice there, it *should* grow—the plants and trees did not bend to his will.

View through Patio and Garden Room

In this early stage of his work, Alex demonstrated an intuitive sense of the minimalist aesthetics of the Japanese concept of Wabi-Sabi. The characteristics of this aesthetic include the idea that beauty is imperfect, impermanent, and incomplete. The overall texture of the House, its fit and finish, reflect a rustic simplicity, here esoteric in its design and execution (Wabi), and the natural weathering of hand-made surfaces that show the effects of time, the imperfect—the peace that comes with acceptance (Sabi). The early House was in harmony with the natural world, and the art and artifacts were understated accents that quietly, like a stone lantern, subtracted nothing from the surrounding voices and images of the natural world. This attitude of working along with nature is more Eastern in spirit as opposed to the then Western (especially American) attitude of contention with, or domination of, the natural world. Alex's restless passion to collect and exhibit would eventually overshadow this aesthetic, but at the very beginning it was clearly there. It is not that Alex studied this aesthetic in a formal way—he knew it intuitively as if he were responding to a universal archetype he could sense within himself. Because of his inborn creative sense, he was able to grasp whole systems with scant evidence—a few illustrations in a book for example—and apply the larger ideas to his own work.

Observation Rock

At the far end of the Patio/Garden is the Grotto which originally featured a statue of St. Francis and later, a hand-carved St. Joseph. Just above the Grotto, the open space of the Garden Room narrows into the more intimate Contemplation Room. In the beginning Alex's mother insisted on religious symbols throughout, even instituting a "Way of the Cross" around the grounds.[29] After his mother's death, Alex removed some religious symbols from The House on the Rock including the "Way of the Cross" but he kept the Grotto and Contemplation Room with its religious statue. Later, he added the Hindu deity shown above the walkway in the previous image "View through Patio and

Garden Room." While he grew away from, and at times even hostile towards, the Catholicism of his youth, he never slipped out of the Catholic milieu in which he was raised and was deeply influenced by his Catholic upbringing—it is a thread that winds its way through all his work.

The rafters that extend out from the roofline of the House are characteristic of The House on the Rock style; this design feature did not come about by accident. Alex liked deep eaves but could not use them on the House because of the high winds that swirl around Deershelter. To create the effect he wanted, he extended the rafters out far past the roof's edge, leading the viewer's eye out beyond the actual edge of the building. Dredging far back into his past we see hints of these rafters in the buildings of Frank Lloyd Wright that he must have seen growing up in Madison, and in Frank Riley's roof rafter treatment at Villa Maria—but this is Alex, so the rafters are stretched and greatly exaggerated.

Rooflines of the House

Alex was conscious of the importance of the entrance to the House. At first it was a rope ladder, then a steep structure part-ladder, part-stairs. Next he designed and built a system more reminiscent of a medieval castle than a house. It was a staircase powered by an electric winch that he could raise and lower from below by a switch locked in a safe built into the rock or from above in the House. If he wanted privacy or security all he needed to do was raise the stairs—a truly private man who wanted to raise the drawbridge against assaults on his privacy. In several relaxed and humorous moments years later with the author in the workshop he conjured up the image of villagers arriving with pitchforks surrounding the House and crying, "Burn the monster!" He was talking and laughing about his excesses in collecting and building in the 1970s but I think it was really how he felt—he needed to raise the drawbridge and be alone.

Alex operating the drawbridge

But Alex was not satisfied with this entrance to the House. He thought it was not dramatic enough, so in 1961 he built the 375-foot flying walkway to the House. This walkway takes visitors from the ground high up through the treetops and satisfied his need for a grand entrance.

Entrance as seen from walkway (after 1961)

An important design technique that Alex liked to employ was the narrowing down of the pathway in which the guests must pass single file in a relatively dark space culminating in an opening up into the light, creating an effect of relief or wonder. This technique is known in architectural circles as compression/expansion and Alex used it repeatedly in his architectural and display work. Author August Derleth described the entrance as "Druid-like," referring to the overpowering rock face that makes up the inner wall at the entrance. This constricted space eventually opens up into the dizzying views through the canted windows of what was once the Living Room, and now is the entrance to The Infinity Room.[30]

Entrance, interior with Carillon in background

Alex was by nature a sculptor. He never seriously turned his attention to drawing and painting although his notebooks contain many working drawings. His early work was three-dimensional. He created several portrait heads of his life partner Jennie that show a beginner's promise, but he never seriously developed his native abilities. In the 1950s he produced a series of "Ming

Horses," and Buddha heads that he and Don Martin cast in Don's basement to make some money. He also produced several small sculptures, one of which survives, a Chinese philosopher riding an ox. Aside from his portrait attempts, the few pieces of work that survive are derivative. Paul Yank, Alex's friend and a successful sculptor himself, thought that Alex could have been a fine sculptor: "I think he would have loved to have been a sculptor, but he couldn't take the time. He lived at a pace beyond everyone. He was on a fast track."[31] This said, sculpture is not something one does—it is what one is. His pushing and pulling, his stretching to the extreme, adding, subtracting, manipulating, discarding, revising of the people and objects around him expose the soul of a sculptor.

Alex with his sculptures

Alex turned his attention to the design and creation of a variety of lamps and ferro-cement casks. There were moments when he proceeded with more considered design, when he took the time, developing original large, rounded forms with extremely thin necks—they were later used as ashtrays in the House. He distributed these works, along with ceramics he collected from local artisans, throughout the House and produced the giant multi-necked pots that became a signature design associated with The House on the Rock. Although at the time, he did described himself as a sculptor, he became more involved in the design and building of the House and he said he simply did not have the time to pursue the art of sculpture any longer. Paul Yank explained: "Alex could have been an architect. He could have been a top contractor. He could have been a sculptor. He could have been any of those things, but he never had time to do that. In a sense, though, he put all those disciplines together in the House."[32]

Multi-neck pot

Some years later, to complement the natural sounds of the birds and the trickle of water throughout the House, Alex had Bob Searles, an artist working for him, put together a program of mood music to accompany visitors on their way through the House. They titled it "The Tales of the Wanderer: Exotic Music of The House on the Rock." The tape recording played softly in the background selections that were meant to evoke travel to exotic lands: "Harbor Lights," "Quiet Village," "The Moon of Manakoora," "Harem Bells," for example set the mood for a "wandering through paradise" as it were.[33]

In the 1950s The House on the Rock became something of a regional gathering place—one of the stops in the shifting venue for a varied group of celebrities, intellectuals, and artists and an invitation to an event at The House on the Rock was sought after. Post-war Madison was filled with returning veterans getting an education under the G.I. Bill, and the University was bustling with creativity. It was a time of great prosperity for the country as well as the beginning of a cultural reawakening. The list of invitees usually centered around the University of Wisconsin Art Department but also included notables from literature, politics, and even sports. Popular University of Wisconsin and NCAA boxing champion Bobby Hinds and Alex became friends and gradually the circle of friends attending widened. Guggenheim Fellow and leading American regional author August Derleth was intrigued by the house, declaring that it was "worked out intuitively, without need of blueprints…a work of indisputable genius."[34] Robert Gard, founder of the Wisconsin Idea Theater visited, famed pianist Gunnar Johannsen played the Steinway, and Governor Gaylord Nelson, one of the founders of the environmental movement, also attended gatherings at The House on the Rock. Members of Frank Lloyd Wright's Taliesin Fellowship, at first leery, eventually came around. Alex had been prevented from participating in World War II, the defining event of his generation, and was the exception among his peer group because he had not served in the military. Some thought that he felt awkward about his lack of military service; it is true that he made a special effort to welcome veterans.

The parties themselves, often including between 125–150 guests, were not organized by Alex himself—he would ask friends to put them together for him. The introverted and shy Jordan would be there but always in the background visiting with everyone; some people came to the events and never knew who he was. Rumors of how wild the parties were are exaggerated. Although the neighbors could clearly hear the loud music, they were actually rather tame affairs described as "having a quietness to them." There was, of course, a bit of carrying on, but mostly they were a gathering of like-minded people out for stimulating conversation and a good time; these events were a chance for Alex to meet interesting people. Lynn Fieldhouse recalled: "He especially had parties around the Fourth of July. Those were the only nights we stayed at the House overnight. He'd have a group of friends, maybe fifteen or twenty, and we'd stay up all night partying. It was marvelous." Alex later reflected, "...No one ever sees the House at its best—at night. I designed the lighting for after-dark effect. It's just unbelievable—breathtaking." He also reflected that the House was "a frightening place to be in a storm."

House exterior

Homer and Lynn Fieldhouse were drawn to Alex and the House in the early years. They heard about Alex and the House just after the property had been purchased from the Christiansons and had to see for themselves so they drove out to visit. They found him planting trees and introduced themselves (Homer was a landscape architect). Alex led them up the ladder to the House and that was the beginning of their friendship. Homer gave Alex a copper pot he had bought at an auction and made a few landscape suggestions, which Alex appreciated. The Fieldhouses and Alex and Jennie spent a lot of good times together going out to eat, dining at the Fieldhouse home, or sitting around talking and drinking. Homer recalled, "In the early years, before he named the House, he and Jennie came over to our house every Saturday night for two years. He'd bring some vodka and we'd do a pretty good job on that. The conversation always got around to what he should name the place. He tried out different names, but he kept referring to The House on the Rock and what he should call it. Finally he looked at me one night and said, 'That must be the name—The House on the Rock.'"[35]

Alex continued to build the House through the 1950s and as time went on the difficult relationship Alex had with his father became more strained and they clashed more often. Alex Sr. was a self-made shrewd businessman who had, through his construction business and his real estate transactions, been able to survive the Depression and prosper in post-war America. When Alex Sr. purchased the land where The House on the Rock now stands it wasn't for recreational purposes, and he had not invested in improvements or hired a full-time employee for the amusement of his son, who was at the time one of his employees. He had something else in mind from the beginning and argued with his son about the future of the House. Alex Sr. saw a business opportunity here, but Junior had a different idea and wanted it to continue as it was—the parties, the good times, and the work. Lynn Fieldhouse remembers, "You see, before it was opened, it was a very personal thing with Alex. At the time his father was pushing him to open it, he wasn't sure he wanted to." The arguments became more frequent, more public, and more heated; Don Martin describes them as "fighting like cats and dogs." After one bitter confrontation Alex reached into his pocket pulled out a handful of coins and said to a friend, "this is what I think of money." He threw the coins off the rock into the woods below. Homer Fieldhouse reflected, "I'd guess it was his father's decision [to open the House]. Alex fought it for a year or two. His father saw all the money going into this place. And to what end? By that time Alex was really building up there." Alex had a sad sense that everything would change if he opened to the public. In 1960, he finally gave in to the inevitable and everything did change. In 1959 feature photo essays about Alex and the House appeared in *The Milwaukee Journal* and *The Wisconsin State Journal* newspapers. The articles included descriptive tours of the House with comments by Alex; if he was trying to keep it private, he was going about it in a strange way.

Ten years later Alex retold the story of the opening of The House on the Rock and cast it in a different light, excluding the conflict with his father and soft pedaling his resistance: "Word got out there was something to see out here, and people began coming around. They'd holler up, 'Can we see your place?' One day we were picnicking and I said, 'By golly, I'm going to charge those folks fifty cents a piece.' And you know they paid gladly. Thanked me even more when they left. We drank real Scotch that night."[36]

That was the end of the parties and other gatherings and the friends associated with this part of The House on the Rock history slowly drifted away. There was one more memorable party the next year as Alex Sr. and Lena celebrated their fiftieth wedding anniversary. They invited a large number of friends and relatives to join them for the day at The House on the Rock. Junior was there too—quietly in the background.

In 1960 motorists along Highway 23 could easily drive by the entrance to the House without knowing it. Alex designed and built, with Don Martin, a towering masonry entrance marker complete with grid-like pergola in The House on the Rock style. They hung a large bell in the masonry and planted vines around the pergola. This was the first "sign" for The House. Later, Alex would design a signboard that they installed at the entrance; this same design was used in hand-made billboards that appeared in the region, nearly the only advertising that he ever did.

Road Entrance (1960)

Everything changed, but with all the visitors came paid admissions and Alex had money to continue to collect and build. Lynn Fieldhouse recalls, "Once he did turn it over to the public, and it got going, it gave him his chance to create even more and further his ideas."[37] He took all the profits and invested them back into The House on the Rock. In 1961 Alex made no additions to the House but designed and built the Gatehouse (see CHAPTER 4). The following year he returned to the House, and this time working with a crew of helpers, he remodeled and enclosed the sun deck, turning it into The Music Room, also used as an art gallery, where he now moved the Steinway. He also expanded his library to extend up through two floors of the building. Above the new Music Room he took the House to its final height building a new deck. When asked if he would build higher he said he thought that he was now about as high as he ought to go, given the general proportions of the House.

Alex was inspired by the work of a favorite poet, Don Blanding, when he wrote:

> "I hope you will come and visit me.
> In The House on the Rock, by the windblown tree,
> For the door open to views beyond.
> For poet, and artist, and vagabond."[38]

CHAPTER 4

GOING PUBLIC

The oral history is that Alex Sr. stood at the top of the stairway with a brown paper bag in his hand and guests deposited fifty-cents admission and that's how it all began. At the time the House was opened to the public it was somewhat smaller than the present House and Alex continued to work on it with his helpers. Income from admissions meant that he could do more, and by 1962 he had completed the building to its present state with the exception of The Infinity Room that was added in 1985.

In 1961 the attraction brought in $34,000 in ticket sales and, for the first time in sixteen years, Alex made no additions to the House. Instead, on a low knoll south of the House he built the Gatehouse. When he was working on the House, Alex proceeded on and around the rock following nature and leaving the terrain undisturbed. In his designs for the Gatehouse he followed the gentle rise and fall of the low knoll, settling the building into the crook of the hill. He left small oaks in place (still thriving today) and sloped the low roof out from the knoll so that it appears to be a natural extension of the hill itself.

Alex's intent in building the Gatehouse was to provide a front entrance for The House on the Rock. He collaborated with designer Dick Hagen on the plan. Alex used what he learned building the House in his work here. Canted windows look out over a terrace extending around the front of the building where Don Martin and crew laid stone walls framing the view of the House and the valley through the trees beyond. It is here that guests get their first taste of the distinctive Jordan style of architecture and the intimate spaces of his interior design.

Fireplaces could never be big enough for Alex, and here he outdid himself with a huge limestone masonry structure including massive iron pots and brass oven doors and a built-in stairway. The low ceilings, gold carpeting, library, and wood finishes are reminders of the House, and here too create an intimate space. The plush built-in seating contrasts with the native limestone masonry. The canted windows, with the exception of the kitchen and entryway windows, are opaque; muted natural light softens the interior space giving the relatively small area an open feeling. There is an easy flow through the interior and out to the atrium and patio. The original design included three bathrooms, an office with its own fireplace, and a working kitchen. He accented the interior of the Gatehouse with artifacts from his growing collections—Asian root carvings, stained glass lamps (in the 1970s) and African tribal art along with examples of the work of local craftsmen. Outside, the low atrium leads to the skywalk (finished in 1961) that carries guests up to the House. It's little wonder that Alex called this his favorite building of all.

His approach in building the Gatehouse was different from The House on the Rock where he built in an impromptu manner following the rock; here he had a clear idea of the whole building from the beginning. He later said, "Although some of the best design work was in the original House, the Gatehouse was the most planned out…." He was also following a contemporary exhibition trend. World's Fairs, such as the New York Worlds Fair of 1939-40 and later the New York 1964-65 and Montreal's Expo '67 incorporated model homes which exhibited the latest (or future) materials, appliances, and architectural designs. In the 1960s Disneyland featured The Monsanto House of the Future. Alex's design was not a house of the future but an architectural and interior design example of the Jordan style; it is a summary of all he had learned presented in a carefully considered plan.

Gatehouse interior

Aside from its model house intent, the Gatehouse was also a practical building housing the main offices and ticket sales as well serving as the entry to the House. On Sundays in summer Alex invited local artists to exhibit their work on the Gatehouse patio; among the well-known artists who showed their works were Harry Nohr, whose wooden bowls have been exhibited at the Smithsonian Institution in Washington. Alex purchased several highly collectible Nohr bowls at this time. Regional ceramic artist Ava Fernekes showed her work as well; Alex later commissioned her to create extraordinary pieces for the Mill House. Although the Gatehouse was finished in 1961, Alex returned to work there in the 1980s when he added a music machine of his own design called "The Gate House Ensemble." In a somewhat mystifying choice of music, he decided to have the theme from Ravel's "Bolero" play un-incrementally over and over again drifting through the Gatehouse and out to the patio and gardens. The Gatehouse today remains just as it was when Alex sat by the fireplace on brisk afternoons.

Alex by the Gatehouse fireplace

On January 1, 1960, Alex P. and Magdalena Jordan created the trade name "The House on the Rock" and the business was listed as a tourist attraction/ showplace. When The House on the Rock Inc. held its first board meeting the notes show Alex Sr. as president, Lena as vice-president, and Alex Jr. secretary, each with 125 shares in the corporation. They opened a business account with American Exchange Bank in Madison. By 1964 they had established a $30,000 line of credit that grew to $250,000 by 1975.

Alex's father now ventured into art collecting after a fashion. In order to increase the reputation of the House, he purchased a number of etchings and engravings by renowned artists; works by Rembrandt, Degas, and Corot, among others, entered the collection of The House on the Rock. These acquisitions were made possible by a Sears Co. marketing program. In an attempt to popularize the arts and make works available to everyone, Sears contracted actor and art collector Vincent Price to oversee and select a large number of etchings, engravings and paintings by famous artists—Sears then sold these to the public. The Madison Sears was one of the stores in the nation-wide program and Alex Sr. bought the works there over a period of several months in 1962.

There is no evidence that he consulted with Alex Jr. in these purchases and they do seem out of character for Junior. At any rate the works were exhibited in the House. The problem with etchings and engravings is that they have no "wall impact;" the masonry walls in the House were not the appropriate venue for them.[39] We cannot know the motivations and the process here, but we do know that sometime after the death of Alex's father in 1963 Alex Jr. removed them all; he did not sell them, but inventoried them and put them in storage where they remain out of public view to this day. Alex was never much taken with two-dimensional work and eventually installed his collection bronzes in the Music Room. His taste was always for sculptural and ceramic forms, objects with weight, objects that displaced space and had a physical impact.

In June 1963 Alex Jordan Sr. died, leaving his Madison property and his shares in The House on the Rock to Lena (she would later sign her husband's shares over to Junior). Lena became president of The House on the Rock, a position she would hold until her death in 1969. After she passed away, Alex became president of the company. The relationship between father and son had been a rocky one; the two Alexes were a study in contrasts. Don Martin recalled, "His dad dressed well. He always wore a white shirt and tie as long as I knew him—Alex [Junior] never wore a tie. He'd wear the same tan corduroy pants 14 days in a row and his shoes were beat-up. You'd swear he never had a nickel in his life. But if that's what made him happy, who's to say he should have been different?" But Don takes the edge off any idea that Alex Sr. was universally unpleasant, reflecting, "His father was a real nice guy, and his mother was wonderful. Alex had the nicest parents a guy could have. Although his mother always told me he had been spoiled since day one. He always got his way."

Alex Sr. was a self-made man who worked hard and struggled through the dark years of the Depression; he had high expectations for his son and passed on to him an entrepreneurial spirit and a never-say-die attitude. It is easy to imagine the conflicts between Alex Sr. the businessman and Alex Jr. the dreamy, creative, restless son. The elder Jordan invested in The House on the Rock enterprise from nearly the beginning demonstrating his belief in Junior's vision, however he may have viewed it. Somewhere inside him, perhaps unspoken, he must have begun to understand the great talents of his son. Alex Jr., whether he reflected on it or not, learned from his father's business acumen and brought to his creative work an underlying practical level-headedness that was a key component of his success.

In the 1960s The House on the Rock was growing rapidly and the business side of the operation became more and more complex. Gladys Walsh was responsible for managing the accounts and the voluminous correspondence of the growing business. She had worked for Alex's parents collecting rents and doing some bookkeeping at Villa Maria. Now she was entrusted with managing the books for The House on the Rock and, even more difficult, providing some order for the mercurial Alex Jr.

Gladys was born in Loyal, Wisconsin in 1899. She was educated at St. Benedict's College and Academy, St. Joseph, Minnesota and attended Eau Claire Teacher's College (later UW-Eau Claire), and Madison Business College. She worked as a proofreader, taught in a country school for a time, worked for The Secretary of State, The Attorney General, and then became a lobbyist in the Wisconsin State legislature. In 1971 the Wisconsin legislature proclaimed her "the people's lobbyist" commending her for "her sincere, vigorous and continuing interest in the laws and government of Wisconsin...." In her spare time she wrote poetry and her collected works were published in 1976 under the title, *A Basket of Sculptured Thoughts*.[40]

For more than twenty years Gladys did the accounting, wrote the checks, composed thousands of letters, press releases, and advertising copy and dealt with government agencies all while keeping an eye on the progress of the company and her unpredictable boss; her work was central to the success of The House on the Rock.

She was sometimes an irritation to Alex and to others who dealt with her because of her persistence and attention to detail. Her record keeping and accounting were meticulous beyond measure. The House on the Rock archives contain bound volumes of copies of all the letters she wrote in response to inquires as well as all business letters. The accounts during her tenure were bound and labeled, every bill, every cancelled check, every letter she wrote, all the daily records are filed—she preserved everything.

Alex was frugal and yet he ignored the fact that she sent employee hand-written time records (some on loose leaf lined paper), and other stuff off to a bookbindery where they were hard bound and labeled in gold print. Looking through the many volumes of bound material in The House on the Rock archives one can't help but conclude that there was something obsessive/compulsive about Gladys. Alex knew this, but he had complete trust in her dedication and honesty and if tolerance for her idiosyncrasies was what it took for him to be at ease about the business end of his enterprise, he considered it well worth the patience that he had to summon to put up with her harmless, if odd, behavior.

As the years went on, Gladys began to show signs of aging; her handwriting became shaky and eventually illegible, her typing (on a manual typewriter) was fraught with uncorrected errors, and she began to make some more serious mistakes. At that time payroll checks were issued from her office and every week and the day after payday employees would line up and present checks with errors, or even checks on which the numbers had been changed using white-out to cover the erroneous figure. Some local banks came to understand and would cash the checks but the situation was becoming anything but humorous. Still, Alex kept her. Once I asked him why, and he said it was because she was old and he hated to get rid of her.

Alex's attorney, John Mitby, describes the elderly Gladys getting a ride across Madison to his office walking on crutches because she had something that Alex wanted him to take a look at. Gradually, a professional firm handled many of the accounts. When Gladys erred by substantially overpaying the IRS, that pretty much signaled the end, and in 1982 Alex replaced her. The sad ending aside, Gladys's dedication to Alex and The House on the Rock and her careful accounting enabled his creative work to continue with confidence and without distraction. Don Martin said of her: "She is the unsung hero of The House on the Rock."

In 1964 Alex was recommended by his friend, landscape architect Homer Fieldhouse, to be in charge of the interior waterfall in the Wisconsin Pavilion for the 1964-65 World's Fair in New York. Alex disliked travel so it was unusual for him to agree to be so far away from home. He may have been enticed to go because of his interest in animation; he heard that Disney was introducing new animation ideas featured in the Mr. Lincoln exhibit. Lynn Fieldhouse said, "Alex was always interested in automation and animation. He had mechanical toys as a boy and that kind of thing just always fascinated him. Not being a traveler, it really surprised me when he went to New York, but it was in part to see Lincoln."[41] He also used the opportunity to visit music machine restorers and dealers, gathering information and planning for the future.

In the nineteenth century, World's Fairs served first as expositions of national pride and later grand displays of science and technology. By the middle of the twentieth century, cultural exchange became the defining idea of World's Fairs. The 1964–65 New York Fair theme was "Peace Through Understanding;" it followed the lead of the 1939–40 New York Fair projecting itself as futuristic and even utopian. Alex was pretty much a country boy dropped down onto this world platform as he worked on the interior of the Wisconsin pavilion—the wonders of the world at his feet, he took it all in. He had an extraordinarily creative and hypersensitive mind able to synthesize new forms and ideas from a variety of stimuli. He was always a keen observer with razor-sharp perception and a broad memory. The New York World's Fair energized Alex. He was effusive in his praise about the speed of construction that he saw at the fair and described the construction site as "awe-inspiring." He reflected on the whole scene, "Unless you saw this wizardry for yourself, it would be difficult to fully appreciate."[42] In his search for rocks for the Wisconsin exhibit he set off driving a truck into Manhattan and eventually ended up going the wrong way down a one-way street. He was pulled over by the police but talked or bumbled his way out of it, playing the part of a rube from the sticks.

But there was time for mischief too, as related by Homer Fieldhouse through author Doug Moe.[43] Alex somehow got a hold of Robert Moses's limousine. Robert Moses, known as "the master builder," was the urban planner who was responsible for shaping New York City's transportation infrastructure in the middle of the twentieth century. He was also the driving force behind, and manager of, the World's Fair. "They had some fun with the car the day before they were to leave New York. The car was equipped with a telephone that was [that day] inoperable.[44] Nevertheless, Jordan had Fieldhouse drove all over the fairgrounds, with Alex in the passenger seat, talking into the phone that didn't work…As they drove along, Jordan, with the phone up to his ear, would call out to workmen, 'Mr. Moses says he would like to see that stand put over there.' He'd point out a location. 'It's very important.' Lynn Fieldhouse says of Jordan, 'There was an impishness about him. He just couldn't resist pulling people's legs at times; most often it was harmless fun.'"

He was not comfortable in the big city in his work clothes. When dress clothes were required he had no choice; his friends took him to Brooks Brothers where he was fitted for a suit. This was the only short period of time when Alex seemed to enjoy more formal attire. Soon he went back to his torn and baggy work clothes. Alex did wear this same suitcoat again (ill-fitting by then) twenty-four years later when he sold The House on the Rock to Art Donaldson.

Alex in his Brooks Brothers suit

He returned home filled with ideas and energy and began a grand expansion of The House on the Rock. With the Gatehouse complete and joined to the House by the treetop walkway, he turned his attention to enhancing the surroundings. Alex was taken with the natural beauty all around him and sought to harmonize his designs with what nature provided.

South of the House, where the first parking lot was, he designed a garden area that he called "The Duck Pond," "The Wildlife Pond," or "The Water Garden." The space was composed of a large outer roofed walkway held up by massive limestone masonry piers. The covered one-hundred-foot oval walkway surrounded the central pond featuring an island refuge for nesting ducks. On the south end of the garden oval a wide waterfall built among the trees and filled with native plants cascaded into the pond. Guests were able to walk under the waterfalls by means of a tunnel that completed the oval walkway. Alex obtained a permit from the Department of Natural Resources to keep a prairie dog colony in an enclosed area attached to the oval. He also installed peacock nests in the piers holding up the walkway to the House but the exotic birds did not last long and fell prey to local four-legged night marauders. Alex called this "a noble experiment." He quipped, "It was originally called the Wildlife Pond, but it became so wild that the foxes came in and ate the ducks. Now we don't have any. We once had a pheasant, but he didn't get out more than a squawk."[45]

Don Martin and Alex built two memorable structures for the garden, one of which survives to this day. First, they spanned the pond area with an intricate spiderweb latticework designed to shade the area and act as an aviary. The design and building of this structure is a tribute to the skill, patience, and seat-of-the-pants engineering of these two autodidacts. Entirely made of wood, it was held in place only by a center post structure. Visitors above on the elevated walkway as well as those below in the garden marveled at the structure. Sadly it collapsed, as did many trees and structures, during the great ice storm of 1976.

The Water Garden interior

The Water Garden latticework

The second, and still-surviving, structure that was designed and built by Alex and Don was The Moongate. The Moongate is a traditional feature of Japanese gardens and was here intended as an entry to the Duck Pond. In addition to its unique part in the Japanese aesthetic of borrowed scenery and framing of the scene beyond, The Moongate was thought to grant good luck to those passing through it. Here Alex makes his boldest quotation of Japanese aesthetics using native limestone to create the round archway.

Just as the project got underway in August of 1964, Alex suffered a severe heart attack. Years of smoking, drinking, and heavy work finally took their toll and now threatened to take his life. He was in the hospital for about a month and his cardiologist reported that, "Following discharge the patient made a dramatic recovery." From this time forward Alex remained on a combination of prescription drugs for treatment of his various ailments including the nitroglycerin tablets he carried with him always. He ended his habit of smoking and quipped that he quit the easy way, "in an oxygen tent." He stopped his excessive drinking but made little effort to change his diet and no attempt at exercise. His health problems continued into the middle 1960s and beyond. In February of 1965 he was re-hospitalized with an acute gallbladder attack but when the symptoms subsided he refused elective surgery; in July of 1966 he developed pneumonia. Through all this he remained focused on his work at The House on the Rock.

With Alex in the hospital after his 1964 heart attack, Don was left on his own to continue The Moongate. By this time Don Martin had become expert in the laying of local limestone that, as usual, he quarried from the property. He recalled that up until this time, "Alex was out [at the House] every day—seven days a week. That made it nice for me—I didn't have to worry if I was on the right track. Sometimes he'd stay for ten minutes, sometimes for three hours. He basically wanted to know how things were going." The Moongate was Alex's idea but as usual there were no plans. This was a challenge of a different sort—it wasn't a wall or a pier; it was round and overhead and he solved the problem by using the same system that ancient and medieval masons had used to construct arches. Don first built a wooden framework shaped like the inner form of the arch. Then he mortared the limestone in place on the form and when the mortar set up he removed the wooden framework and he had his arch. Don always viewed this work with great pride and when asked if Alex liked it when he returned from the hospital he answered demurely, "Well he didn't tear it down." Actually Alex very much approved of The Moongate, as a newspaper photograph taken soon after shows—the post heart attack Alex, thinner, in his Brooks Brothers suit, smiling proudly as he posed in front of The Moongate.

Alex in front of The Moongate

The Moongate design marks a departure point for Alex as he now moved away from any reference to Japanese aesthetics. The Asian design quotations begun in the House twenty years before found an ending here at The Moongate. He was now moving in an entirely different direction. As if to bring everything full circle, he returned to The Moongate twenty years later to create a small Zen garden there a few weeks before he died.

CHAPTER 5

THE TRANSITION

The Mill House opened in 1968 after two years of construction but the plans had been in Alex's mind for years. Alex asked his friends to put down some of their, and his, ideas on paper and several drawings exist (none of which he followed). In the end, he went about it as usual with the plan in his head and daily directions for the workmen. He said that the building, "Started out to be oriental and ended up being medieval." The very idea of the Mill House is a summoning up of nostalgic images of times gone by and speaks to his romantic bent. In his familiar style, Alex used massive timbers and native limestone for the structure and relied on his right-hand man Don Martin for the masonry and carpentry. Don said at the time, "I've laid miles and miles of stone that we quarried on our own place and near by, including the seven tiers of the circular stone wall just completed around the new Duck Pond." The attention to detail in this building is typical Jordan, from the hand-hewn support columns, roof joists, and beams, to the wooden pegs and the fourteen-foot, handmade waterwheel—everything has the Jordan stamp on it.

The sod roof was kept in trim by a goat named Lucifer and the wooden raceway complete with gates seemed to disappear into the hillside. In the spring of 1968 the pond was filled and the wheel began to turn, greased with tallow from a local butcher. Alex always identified with his Swiss heritage and studied illustrations of Swiss alpine buildings perusing a large old book containing numerous engraved illustrations of the Swiss bucolic countryside; he referred to this book as The Bible. The sod roof, the goat, and the low rooflines are further romantic references to Switzerland. Later he would gather artifacts to construct a building-sized cuckoo clock and cover other buildings with sod roofs held in place by faux rocks. He had sculptures created depicting the Wilhelm Tell story and placed them on the waterfalls in the garden as well as sculptures of Swiss figures playing alpenhorns—long wooden horns used in mountainous regions of Switzerland as a means of communication.

The Mill House exterior

The fireplace size and design that was not possible in The House on the Rock itself was finally achieved in the Mill House. He claimed it was the largest fireplace in the world, thirty-four-feet long, complete with stone steps and a spiral staircase; it was patterned, according to Alex, after one in a Scottish castle and he spread the word that there was a secret room hidden away up the staircase—that was show biz; there never was such a room. In another version explaining the stairway in the fireplace he claimed it led to a smokehouse. The massive fireplace contains a number of copper cheese vats originally used in the manufacture of Swiss cheese and a wooden winch and iron chain for hauling tree trunks into the fireplace where they were burned on chilly spring and fall days.

The Mill House fireplace

The stone floor and rough walls are reminders of the ambiance of the House. The Mill House served as a transitional building for Alex. It is still within the style and materials that he used in the House itself as well as the Gatehouse, but the Mill House is more reminiscent of a bygone era. Although the textures and materials are similar to his previous work, it is here that he began to experiment with designs for the exhibition of his growing collections. Gone are the low ceilings and canted windows. The design relates almost exclusively as an interior. The interior and exterior of the building relate only through the windows at the entrance that overlook the spinning millwheel.

On the interior, the doll shop, and his toy bank and gun collections mark his first attempt to display collections in a themed environment. Until now he displayed artifacts as one might in a home, on shelves or in niches just out of the reach of the public. He didn't want to create displays in the museum tradition and the Mill House offered an opportunity for him to experiment. Here for the first time he used dramatic lighting to display artifacts and to create dark and mysterious corners and rich textured color. The Bates taxidermy collection dating from before 1880 struck Alex especially because it contains birds (a golden eagle and owls) that were now against the law to mount. This appealed to his need for the curiously exotic that would make his collections remarkable; he also enjoyed seeming to be slightly outside the law.

His interest in gun collecting was evident early on and several antique long rifles were on display in the original House in the 1940s and 1950s. A good collection became available in the 1960s when Ira Moody of Moody's Musical Museum in McGregor, Iowa, decided to quit business. Alex had long been familiar with the museum where he listened to a variety of music machines and periodically visited the eclectic collection of memorabilia including dolls, guns, carriages, and music boxes. During the middle 1960s Ira sold Alex a large number of artifacts, many of which ended up in the Mill House collections, including suits of armor, a doll collection, a variety of guns, and music machines. The core of the collection of guns came from Moody's and is presented in a fairly straightforward manner, arranged in glass cases framed in rustic wood under low light; Alex added to the collection from his own stock and also created several fantasy pieces. The display was later featured in the July 1971 issue of *Guns* magazine.

Alex was conscious from the beginning of the need to appeal to both male and female sensibilities; he acquired a huge bellows and turned it into a glass-topped table that housed his glass paperweight collection, and he stood the suits of armor in built-in wood and glass cases. He installed his newly refurbished music machines: The Hupfeld Phonoliszt Violina, an early twentieth-century German orchestrion, dubbed "the eighth wonder of the world," and the Regina Sublima, an American upright metal disk music box from the 1890s, a machine he got from Moody's Museum. The Hupfeld was acquired from a West Coast dealer who found it in Fallbrook, California. Alex paid a mere $600 for what would become a world-class treasure.

The beginnings of his new approach can be seen in his treatment of the doll collection. He came up with an idea that seems incongruous—a storefront display built into the architecture of the building. The Paragon Toy Co. is incorporated into the far corner of the building and makes possible the display of his growing doll collection. It is a creative solution that served two purposes: first, it provided a unique display space in which the dolls and other artifacts can be seen in a storefront setting. The rustic mullions of the low windows and the obstructed view make viewers look around the interior, moving and craning their necks to see it all—there is a sense of discovery and a need to point out to friends things they may have missed. And here, as in his future work, he includes little accent pieces, unexpected treasures to find. Secondly, it gave Alex a chance to experiment with interior storefront design in preparation for his next major project, where he would expand this concept into an entire environment, The Streets of Yesterday.

The Paragon Toy Shop in the Mill House

And then there was the unexpected. One day Alex showed up with some glassware and explained to the workmen how to build window displays and use the glassware to create a wall of glass for the interior of the women's restroom. He commissioned artist Ava Fernekes to create whimsical ceramic sculptures for the displays in the restroom as well. Ava and her husband Max were frequent visitors to The House on the Rock; they were the first artists to move to nearby Mineral Point that gradually turned into something of an artist's colony. In the men's restroom he built a display of model trains and steam engines. This is the beginning of a feature that The House on the Rock is famous for all over the world—themed bathrooms. Others would eventually create their own themed bathrooms, but Alex Jordan's Mill House bathrooms are the start of it all; they are part of a unique House on the Rock tradition. Men and women often come out of their respective bathrooms and urge partners to come with them into their bathroom to see the displays—a unique, if sometimes slightly embarrassing experience.

Window in women's restroom, Mill House

The end of the 1960s marked not only a transition in Alex's creative life but also important changes in his personal life. In April of 1969 Alex's eighty-year-old mother Lena passed away. Since the death of Alex Sr. in 1963 she and Alex held all of the shares in The House on the Rock Inc., and now those shares passed to Alex, making him the sole owner. By all accounts, Mama J., as she was known in the family, was a strong woman with her feet planted firmly on the ground. She was reputedly not given to showing her feelings and was staunchly religious. She bore up under the reported philandering of her husband and the misbehaviors of Alex Jr., telling her friend Esther Korb, "Oh Esther, the two greatest thorns in my side are my two Alexes."[46] She carried with her always a picture of Florence, her baby girl who had died in 1913.

The record of the archival material she left behind shows that she did not follow the subservient role associated with women of her time but was involved with the family business on a daily basis. A key ingredient in Alex's success was his grasp of the details of his business; he grew up in a household where economy, orderly and detailed record keeping, and well-thought-out financial transactions were the norm. Lena for her part carried on the entrepreneurial tradition and business spirit of her father, George Pregler. The Jordans had advanced themselves through hard work but not without hard times and this served as a lesson Alex took with him throughout his life.

Lena had very high expectations for Alex Jr. and was disappointed that Junior did not follow her lead in religious faith, behaved poorly, and even brought shame on the family with his misadventures. He learned from her those very important lessons of stubborn hard work, economy, and attention to detail, that served him so well in his life. In the end, she had lived long enough to see her son's unique creative spirit and share in his vision. As the 1970s began, Alex Jordan was his own man and he was on the verge great success.

Those who had dealings with Alex usually underestimated his knowledge and understanding. He had a disarming appearance with his baggy pants and torn shirt, pens and notepads crammed into his breast pocket and wallet stuffed thick with notes and a large amount of cash rumored to be as much as $10,000. Gladys Walsh handled all the details of the accounting; at first Alex would collect all the day's receipts in a bag and take them to her in Madison, she would count it, and he would later carry it to the bank in a money belt. When receipts became larger, he carried them to a local bank bringing them from the office to his vehicle in a lunch box looking like a laborer heading home—later he needed a shopping bag. In 1970 income totaled $380,000 and by the middle of the decade had exceeded one million and climbing. All of this he reinvested in The House on the Rock while he continued to live his simple lifestyle.

Tourism and its impact on the economy was not yet a developed study, but Alex read everything he could find on the subject, clipping and saving stacks of articles from newspapers and magazines. He tracked attendance and gate receipts daily and used the data to compare years, also keeping track of and recording daily weather as well as the dates of holidays that might impact his business. Most importantly, he stayed in contact with visitors to The House on the Rock; he did this the way any shy man would—anonymously. Dressed as the workman he was at heart, he could often be found sitting on a masonry wall at the entrance to the ticket area watching and listening to the visitors as they came and went sometimes striking up a conversation, "Well, what do you think of all this?" This was his market research. On the occasions when guests would recognize him or guess at his identity he would say, "No, I'm not Alex Jordan, I'm just the plumber." Or "No, that's my brother, I'm just a carpenter." Throughout his life at The House on the Rock he always found time to circulate among the visitors and listen to their reactions. Sometimes he felt the need to break out of his anonymity; one day he was watching guests pass through one of the turnstiles when a large woman approach and couldn't get through. In a fit of rudeness, he piped up, "Get out of here, you're too fat to be here." It was *his* place, and he certainly felt he could do exactly as he liked—a fact never more telling than the day an older woman leaned in to the ticket seller after purchasing her tickets and said, "Listen, I don't want to cause trouble, but there's a homeless man urinating in the parking lot."[47]

The phenomenal growth of his business was not accidental but the result of a perceptive reading of public reaction, the economic use of resources, and his creative entrepreneurial spirit.

CHAPTER 6

FINDING THE NEW WAY

The Mill House was not yet finished, and Alex was already working on an entirely new project—The Streets of Yesterday, a recreation of a nineteenth-century American street in great detail, filled with period antiques and reproductions. He studied other attractions that displayed artifacts in a street setting: The Henry Ford Museum in Dearborn, Michigan and the Milwaukee Public Museum among others.

The Streets represent a new phase of Alex's creativity; up until this point he was interested in making architectural statements as he had done in the House, the Gatehouse, the Mill House and the Water Garden. Now he turned his attention to creating works that were interior design themes of a theatrical nature. This shift also parallels an inward turning of his already reserved personality and a gradual closing off of the outside world. As his work became more popular and the crowds increased, threatening his privacy, he turned away, taking refuge inside himself and shrinking his small circle of associates. Through the 1960s the old connections formed when the House was a gathering place faded away and he focused on his work and increasingly associated only with those directly connected with his business. Although he would return to architecture in 1985 with the addition of The Infinity Room to complete the House, his work now consisted of creating interior environments. Remarkably, in the early 1970s, to gain control of the lighting in the House he covered the canted windows with blue Plexiglas and achieved dramatic low lighting for the installation of a collection of custom-made-Tiffany-style lamps. The breathtaking and sometimes dizzying panorama from the overhanging windows was shut out and something of the airy light and pleasure of encroaching nature was lost—

his attention was turning inward, an inward turn that paralleled the limiting of his socialization. It was also at this time that he began to build screening panels at various locations along the exterior pathway of the tour to hide from view some of the growing number of huge metal buildings that had begun to sprawl down the hillside under the House. In the next decade he would fill these structures with the wonders of his imagination. His need to control every aspect of the tour became more pronounced and he was conscious of every detail of display design and lighting as he sought to increase the sense of wonder and mystery in the experience of The House on the Rock.

Don Martin reflected about his work with Alex on the Mill House: "I think that Alex had it in the back of his mind, though he never told me, that he was building a fun entrance [at the Mill House] to The Streets of Yesterday even then." Alex had been visiting the Milwaukee Public Museum for some time by then, asking Don to go with him but Don—ever the country boy—never did go. The Milwaukee Museum is famous the world over for its exhibits, especially its dioramas. Paul Yank, who worked as a sculptor at the museum from 1958 to 1969, was at work on a diorama one day in 1960 when he noticed a big man nosing around the displays and watching him. Finally Alex introduced himself saying that he had a place west of Madison and started asking questions about diorama building and the creation of artificial rock formations. After they talked for a while, Paul took him down into the basement of the museum and showed him around, and that was the beginning of their friendship. Paul shared his knowledge with Alex, explaining the techniques that he used in his work. He recalls: "He was a master working with materials. As the House was developing he'd want to know how some of the different things we were doing were made. We got into doing fiberglass with some of our figures, to make them lighter, so they'd be put more easily in motion. I showed him how we were doing it."[48]

In the 1960s the Milwaukee Museum was creating a nostalgic exhibit called "Streets of Old Milwaukee" which turns out to be where the germ of the idea for Alex's Streets of Yesterday came from. As usual, Alex read everything he could to prepare for this new project. Yank reflects on Alex's process: "He'd get pictures. He'd get all the information he could. It's what I did at the museum. I told him you had to be a historian also, you research and you research and when you've got all you can, you do it." And Alex did do his research in reference books and old Sears and Roebuck catalogues that he pored over for hours, finding illustrations of artifacts from a bygone era.

Don Martin was in charge of the carpentry and construction and the general management of the project and says he truly enjoyed himself, recalling: "You see, by that time I was getting to be more of a carpenter." In the spring of 1970 Alex hired Bob Searles to help with the design and detailing of The Streets of Yesterday. Before coming to work for Alex, Bob was the curator of Villa Louis, a Victorian era mansion located on the Mississippi River and run by the State Historical Society of Wisconsin. He brought an eye for detail, love of antiques, an appreciation of historic buildings, and his artistic skills to the Streets project.

The Streets of Yesterday under construction

Like so many other artists and craftspeople who worked for Alex, he counts the experience as seminal in his growth as an artist. He went on to become a well-known porcelain sculptor and attributes his success in great part to his experience working with Alex, calling his stay at The House on the Rock, "The most life-changing 834 days of my life." Working for Alex was a challenge every day; he was driven and insistent on production at the quality level that he wanted, relentless, quick to show his displeasure and often slow to praise. Bob says further, "The courage to pursue this career [porcelain sculpture] would never have surfaced if I had not had the experience of working for and with Alex Jordan at The House on the Rock...."[49] Craftspeople had to come in, day in and day out, and produce, work out the problems on their own—no excuses. It was that expectation and the pressure that Alex applied to the work, the stretching of ideas and materials that allowed those who could deal with him to grow in their craft. And being in on the design and planning was a life experience that cannot be duplicated. Bob is one of the many grateful artists who worked with Alex over the years.[50] While Alex was imperious by nature he still needed active and talented collaborators and often the final product of his initial vision was the result of a great deal of input from artisans and craftspeople with a lot of pushing and pulling on his part.

In the Streets project, Alex had a general scheme in mind and some clear ideas about the direction he was going. In Don Martin's words, "We just went up one side of the street and down the other," building one structure after another. First, the building to house the Streets was constructed, and then work began on the first structure, Grandma's House, at one end of the building. As usual, the plans were in Alex's head and he changed and added as he went along from building to building; this creative and flexible approach resulted in freshness in the design and detail of The Streets of Yesterday. Other examples of this genre are often built on a flat surface in a regular grid-like pattern resulting in a lifeless lack of warm ambience, whereas Alex's Streets curve into the distant darkness creating an expectation of discovery. The brick street follows the natural slope of the land, rising and falling over the irregular terrain and encourages visitors walking in the Streets to slow down and look. To create the illusion of larger buildings in a confined area the scale of the structures was altered, especially the second stories; this combined with nighttime lighting adds to the illusion. The ambience allows for a leisurely stroll past the Barber Shop, Jail, Apothecary, Ferdie Wirth's Lamp Store, J.P. Richman's luxury home, Fire Engine Company No. 1, etc. Within the Streets he installed part of his exotic collection of animations: the fortuneteller Esmerelda, a French antique animated magician, and The Dying Miser among them.

View up the Streets

In 1971 when the Streets opened to the public, Paul Yank visited and remarked, "It's authentic, the craftsmanship is wonderful. Some of Alex's re-creations are superior to those at good museums...Alex really tried to get it right..." But he didn't get it right using the cold logic of a lifeless museum, or the sugarcoated Main Street (McStreet) of Disney. Alex's Streets came together as an impromptu and singular vision and there was no one bugging him about schedules or budgets or plans—this was not something that could be done by a committee. As a result, The Streets of Yesterday are alive, replete with limitless detail and filled with the unexpected. One of the visitors who summed it up was businessman Art Donaldson: "It's entertaining, it's alive, it's not like a museum. It does something to everyone who goes there. It gets into their soul...." Near the end of his life in 1988, Alex sold The House on the Rock to Art.[51]

About this time Alex started collecting nineteenth-century horse-drawn vehicles; he included these in the Streets and filled the buildings with period antiques as well as the reproductions he had been collecting for years. He was beginning to become known as a collector, and people with antiques to sell often sought him out. One of the collectors he associated with in the 1960s was Pete Burno, engineer and collector of steam-operated engines. As a dramatic exclamation point at the end of the Streets Alex had Pete install an enormous steam tractor that he drove to its final destination under steam power with Bob Searles acting as fireman. This "landlocked leviathan" was then equipped with wooden fenders, a lighted canopy and a sign declaring: "Peter H. Burno Mighty in Strength and Endurance."

The Calliope and the Burno Steam Tractor

Whether it was Grandma's House, J.P. Richman's elegant residence, or anything in between, Alex looked at The Streets of Yesterday as visual pleasure for visitors and nothing else and often said about guests, "Don't educate them— entertain them." As it turns out, guests find the pleasant ambience of The Streets of Yesterday both entertaining and educational.

The standard of the amusement industry at the time of the building of The Streets of Yesterday was Walt Disney. Jordan and Disney were polar opposites and had very different approaches and created very different worlds of entertainment. Walt Disney was outgoing, gregarious, and enjoyed nothing more than seeing people have a good time. Alex Jordan was pretty much monosyllabic and reclusive, a showman like Disney, but an illusionist trickster whose dark side was close to the surface. Walt himself was not all fun and games, being dubbed "The Dark Prince of Hollywood." The well-groomed Main Street in Disneyland invites the visitor to return to childhood, or the illusion of childhood, in a too perfect environment. Neal Gabler writing in *Disney: The Triumph of The American Imagination* says that Disneyland is, "Too serene, too clean, too controlled, too perfect...It was what one might have called 'the tragedy of perfection'—that in seeking perfection Walt seemed to drive out anything human and real." And further, "It was a modern variant of the City on a Hill of Puritan dreams. It was the consummate act of wish fulfillment."[52] Disney, in his Main Street and throughout his amusement parks, has been accused by some of taking the edge and danger out of his art.[53]

In Jordan's work in The Streets of Yesterday and throughout The House on the Rock we see both playful, child-like excitement and a darker side where desire and brooding imagination rule—not always a comforting place to be. Guests don't participate in Alex's world as they do in Disney's and are not engaged as in an amusement park. Alex is not expecting viewers to lose themselves in childhood memories (or the fabrication of same) and immerse themselves in a perfect world—we are merely fascinated observers. The House on the Rock has more in common with ancient Cabinets of Curiosities, "Ripley's Believe it or Not"®, or P.T. Barnum's American Museum than with Disney's creations. Alex's guests never fall into the rabbit hole of an illusory world, and he has left some of the edge on, installing enough dark allusions and haunting desire to keep their feet firmly, if uncomfortably, on the ground. Disney's Street is meant to transport the guest to a perfect dreamy time and place, while Jordan's is about looking in from the outside at a halcyon age filled with desire, hinting at tragedy, and always conscious of the human condition.

Among the dolls, magic lanterns, and toy trains in the Victorian Grubb's toy shop in The Streets of Yesterday is an example of the edge he has left on: in an obscure corner is a glass bottle containing a doll funeral complete with coffin, flowers and mourners, a dark *memento mori*—no perfect illusory world here. Throughout the attraction, Alex often accented his exhibits with reminders of death, for example in the figure of Death in the Four Horsemen of the Apocalypse (one of his favorites) and the extraordinary collection of horse-drawn hearses he gathered for future displays. He put them there to shock his guests but perhaps also as a talisman to ward off the inevitable—whistling past the graveyard.

A look at the boudoir of Kitty du Bois, built later in The Music of Yesterday, is evidence that Alex was not intending to create a wholesome dream world or that he had any fear of getting too close to the edge, just as the kitschy bare-breasted female mannequins all over the Carousel Room ceiling tell you you're not in Disneyland.

Alex is always lurking in the shadows of his work waiting for us to dig deeper. In Grubb's Toy Shop the Devil puppet slouches languidly on the shelf above the doll funeral; it is a vision of the far-off world of Victorian childhood with simple charming toys, but underneath Alex has made sure that the Dickensian side of that era is there too. Part of the Jordan collection of nineteenth-century miniature animated tableaus is installed at various locations in the Streets and elsewhere, "The Death of the Miser," and "The Dying Drunkard" among them. These antique, moralistic scenes fascinate, and occasionally creep out, modern viewers—Alex understood the deeper allusion at play here. "The Death of the Miser" was inspired by a 1490 painting by Hieronymus Bosch, a painter Alex was very familiar with and whose aesthetic sense contributed to Alex's ideas for the Inferno Room designs (See CHAPTER 9); the tableau is not just a jab in the ribs but also turns out to be a reference to a late medieval work—entertainment in a minor key. The Electric Belt display located outside the Apothecary Shop is vintage Jordan; it just seems like a bit of early twentieth-century quackery and worth not much more than a glance. A longer look reveals how it would work—it has to do with electricity and gonads. He's there, the bad boy, laughing with us. The Streets are Jordan at his best.

Walt Disney's long-time animator Ward Kimball confided, "If you want to know the real secret of Walt's success, it's that he never tried to make money. He was always trying to make something he could have fun with or be proud of." Much the same was true of Alex Jordan.

They may have had more very deeply in common than we might at first think. Much has been made among behaviorists of Disney's domineering, disapproving and remote father and the unhappy environment of his early years resulting in his desire to construct a perfect reflection of an imaginary childhood. The Dark Prince certainly did carry a lot of baggage. Alex Jordan's father reputedly fit this model. Alex's darker, deeper motivation for creating his own nostalgic world that we are allowed to view but not enter, and in which he is somewhere there hiding behind the scenes, can only be speculated upon. It is not within the scope of this book or the expertise of this author to follow these pathways, but it is food for thought.

At the far end of the Streets he built the Gladiator Calliope, as you can see in the image "The Calliope," and began, with this music machine, a new period of creation more innovative and astounding than anything he had done before. While the Streets were still under construction in the early 1970s Alex turned his attention to a new project, The Music of Yesterday.

Alex started collecting band organs, orchestrions, and music boxes and later pipe organs in the 1960s and began to develop vague ideas about how he was going to use them. He researched the history and construction of music machines, joined The Music Box Society, and picked up all the information he could from fellow collectors and dealers. He began to visit Svoboda's Nichelodeon Tavern and Museum on the south side of Chicago where he studied the largest collection of orchestrions, coin-operated pianos, and band organs on display anywhere. While he was working at the World's Fair in New York in 1964, he made it a point to visit band organ dealers. The concept of what he was going to do was gradually forming in his mind and Alex became well known among band organ dealers and collectors as he expanded his collection. He listened to every recording of band organs he could get his hands on. By 1970 he had amassed barns full of church and theater organs from all over the country—these would be part of the raw material for where he was heading next.

These instruments were in constant need of adjustment and repair so Alex contracted qualified organ repair people to service his machines. Dave Ramey came to The House on the Rock to work on the machines, and soon they were planning a new machine of their own. He called it The Gladiator Calliope and positioned it at the far end of the Streets. Alex was famously frugal and brought in junk parts wherever he found them and had Dave combine these with spare organ components he picked up, eventually running the whole contraption off an organ paper roll mechanism. Alex added his own decorative touches to their experiment that later included animated figures, indulging his life-long fascination with automatons—these figures were his first attempt to create animations of his own. The public was enchanted with this machine, much to Alex's delight, and that was the beginning of a new venture that he called The Music of Yesterday.

The Calliope

He made pages and pages of entries in his notebooks in the form of long lists and drawings, exploring not only design but also the mechanical workings of various components. His creative process was always flexible and drew from all the sources around him; he changed the concept as he went along and took suggestions from his artisans and technicians (sometimes forgetting where the idea had come from). The final work was a result of this dynamic creative process. He allowed the public to see and hear his creations only when he was satisfied and then applied what he called "the ten minute test." Greg Burke, who worked with Alex beginning in the late 1970s and ended up as manager of The House on the Rock in Alex's final years explained: "It wasn't whether he liked an exhibit or not, or whether we liked it, he had a ten minute test. If it was well received in the first ten minutes after a project was done and the room was open, well that was the response we lived with. He wanted to hear, 'Oh, wow! That's fantastic!' If he heard that, it was a success for life."[54] Usually he got the reaction that he wanted. If by the end of ten minutes they weren't awestruck, he felt he had failed. He returned to work and altered the exhibit (even making radical changes) until he got the reaction he expected. Then he was finished—but he was never completely finished and returned to many of his creations, in some cases years later, to make changes. While he did value the end product of his efforts—after all the work brought about more admissions and more money to create yet more wonders—he was more interested in the act of creation. He would never be done—creation was not what he did—it was who he was.

It nearly all came to a screeching halt in December of 1972 when Alex had a near-fatal car accident. He was an impatient and fast driver; one day in 1972 he was nearly killed when he broadsided a horse. He said, "That damn horse's timing couldn't have been better if we had planned it together. The car was totaled and so was I, just about. I fractured my skull, jaw and leg in that one. Oh, yeah, and my neck too. I was a quadriplegic for a while."[55] In fact, doctors did not expect him to live. The nurses had given up and thought that he would surely die. Some of them were even reluctant to enter his room. Jennie came every day, stayed with him, dressed his injuries and nursed him back from the brink.[56] He was hospitalized for just over two months. From his hospital bed he continued to create, asking that his workmen visit him in the hospital to report in and get instructions—his recovery was slow.

His heart condition, diabetes, car accident, and football injuries from his high school days slowed his body down. He was never far from pain and medication for the rest of his life. As the years went on, Alex suffered circulation problems in his extremities; his injuries caused a partial deformity of his hands and he began to walk with a slight shuffle. Workers were amazed when he occasionally tested electrical circuits by poking his finger in an open light socket saying he felt, "just a little tickle."

He returned to work slowed and lacking the old stamina. Alex hired a driver who took him back and forth to the House until the day when he said he could drive himself. Through all of it he was absorbed in The Music of Yesterday.

The Music of Yesterday is a labyrinthine walk that narrows (compresses) and opens up (expands) into a series of intimate musically themed environments. The ever-faithful Don Martin was the master mason and in charge of general construction. The new member of the team was John Hovancak who in years to come would go on to become a renowned restorer of rare music machines. For John, as for so many craftspeople, this challenging work with Alex was a learning experience where he perfected his craft but not without some pain and conflict. A man with the ideals of a master craftsman soon learned that there was the right way of doing things, and there was Alex's way of doing things, and there was the road; Alex's way was going to win in the end. Used parts, junk parts, parts he had to invent, silly ideas that Alex had, and brilliant challenges—the wonder is that is spite of it all, the machines that they built were showstoppers that caused visitors to burst into applause. John's contribution to The Music of Yesterday is one of the most extraordinary works of craftsmanship in the history of The House on the Rock.

Alex approached this project with original thinking, literally thinking outside the box. Band organs were basically fancy boxes with organ pipes and percussion arranged inside and sometimes attached to the outside. Music is produced on the same basic principle as a player piano controlled by a paper roll. Alex was not satisfied with the limits of the band organs he owned or had listened to; he had a better idea. He wanted to get rid of the box and install the musical instruments in themed rooms with the instruments spread around. He also wanted to add animated instruments and effects that aped musical sounds produced by ranks of hidden pipes. The control mechanisms in the beginning remained paper rolls but later as his demands became more complex they graduated to electronic systems. The Music of Yesterday opened in 1974 but Alex kept adding to the displays all of his life and one, The Blue Danube, was completed after he passed away.

As he progressed, Alex adapted more modern methods in creating his machines, switching from paper-roll mechanisms to electronic recording devices and finally to simple computer systems. Increasingly, he began to add synthesized music to his creations to achieve just the effects he wanted. The music machines Alex created should be viewed as performance pieces in theatrical settings and although he used salvaged mechanisms, pipes, and other parts from band organs, he was departing from tradition. What he understood was the deeply sensual nature of the effects he was trying to achieve; if an antique music machine suited his purposes he installed it in a pleasing setting, but restoring ancient music machines was not his goal—he left that to others.

Among all the machines he created, three from the middle 1970s are prime examples of his work: Kitty's Room, The Blue Room, and The Mikado.

Peering over the railing into Kitty's Room, the boudoir of "renowned New Orleans entertainer" Kitty du Bois, guests find the instruments arranged around the brass bed with overhead mirror, nightgown casually draped over the bedstead, red velvet upholstery, and hookah water pipe, and once the music starts so do the smiles. This music machine was built from scratch in the workshops. A saxophone in the light of a Tiffany style lamp picks up the honky-tonk strains of Boots Randolph's "Yakety Sax." Here Jordan ventured as far as he thought he could along the edges of the murky land of eroticism. He knew his audience well. The truth is that guests of all persuasions enjoy discovering the odd puerile moment as they make their way through elbowing each other, pointing and giggling, and it turns out that this feature was for him an important part of the show. Alex often called on his adolescent, child-like self as he sought to titillate or mildly shock his guests with suggestive settings like Kitty's, scantily clad sculptures, or naked breasts throughout the complex, usually staying clear of kitsch but occasionally spilling over.

Kitty's Room

In the late 1970s the author, at Alex's direction, created a particularly voluptuous female figure for him and asked about the danger of offending the public, especially little old ladies, Alex replied, "Those little old ladies are a lot tougher than you think." Be that as it may, there were only occasional objections that Alex dismissed with a sniff saying "We don't want people like that around here." At any rate, Alex was in touch with his audience and never pushed the envelope much beyond the veiled sexual allusions of The Boudoir of Kitty du Bois. Sexuality was never the main theme of Alex's work but it is an underlying feature that reoccurs as an accent here and there.

Queen Victoria's railroad coach was reportedly the inspiration for The Blue Room completed with John Hovancak in 1975; that may have been the starting point, but Alex was too improvisational and eclectic to follow any period design theme. As was his habit, he filled pages of his notebooks with ideas and sketches for The Blue Room as the idea began to develop. The mirrored room with its crystal chandeliers, blue velvet wall covering, Louis Quatorze faux furnishings and exotic statuary is a window into a romantic vision reminiscent of Bavaria's mad King Ludwig, rather than homage to the excesses of the dour Victoria. The musical ensemble is an unconventional chamber orchestra with strings, woodwinds, keyboard, percussion, and, go figure, marimba—all animated and/or playing. The blue velvet curtains at the rear of the room concealed the brains and musical source of many of the sounds in the form of an antique music machine. Alex had a preference for classical music, although his listening habits were somewhat broader; here in The Blue Room he indulged that taste including one of his favorite works, "The Poet and Peasant Overture" by Franz von Suppé. The Blue Room was his first attempt at the use of classical music in his original music machines and the public response was very favorable. The collaboration between Alex and John Hovancak continued as they made their way further into the project.

The Blue Room

The high-water mark of the relationship between John and Alex was the 1976 production of the most popular music machine in the collection, The Mikado. It began with the acquisition of a Mortier orchestrion. Mortier was an organ manufacturer based in Belgium where the company produced a large number of organs before ceasing business in 1948. Alex's passion for music machines prompted his only trip outside the U.S. In 1971 he visited Belgium to learn more about band organs. He was also no doubt aware of the political situation developing in Belgium at the time and the growing national movement to stop the export of cultural artifacts, including band organs. He stayed only one day and it is rumored that when asked if he would like to take a side trip to the Rembrandt Museum in Amsterdam he said he wanted to get back home.

John restored the Mortier and Alex directed the addition of a number of extra instruments to achieve the effect he was after. He decided on an Oriental theme and the name "Mikado" after the Gilbert and Sullivan comic opera of the same name. He searched his sources in Chicago, Jo Mead artifacts and the wholesale outlet Merchandise Mart among them, from whom he acquired the statues, birdcages, lamps, and exotic bric-a-brac that went into the project. As the machine came together the Mortier disappeared behind layer after layer of red and gold oriental sculptures and artifacts. Alex also pursued his interest in automatons, including two seated figures with animated features, one playing the kettle drum moving his head and eyes and the other puffing his cheeks as he blows into a complex bamboo wind instrument. The animation here is greater in complexity than his first attempts in the Calliope in The Streets of Yesterday and was to be the high point of his work with John. Drawing once again from classical sources Alex chose the music: Camille Saint-Saens' "Danse Macabre," and "The Ritual Fire Dance" by Manuel de Falla and "Harem Bells," a choice inspired by Alex's familiarity with the work of one of the strangest entertainers of the era, Korla Pandit. It was pure entertainment and the audience loved it, often breaking into applause at the end of songs. He had amazed them again. Not long after The Mikado began to play, John moved on to new horizons.

The Mikado

Alex always had plans for new music machines and left a number of them unfinished at the time of his death in 1989. Neil Hanson and John Kraus finished the "Blue Danube" and the "Circus Orchestra" working from the instructions Alex had given them and building the remainder based on their years of experience working with Alex.

Alex's love of music was not limited to his work; he became a significant sponsor of The Symphony of the Hills, a summer festival of the arts featuring a youth symphony and the Coulee Region Symphony. The festival culminated every year with a concert at nearby Governor Dodge State Park that always ended with one of Alex's favorites, "The 1812 Overture" complete with fireworks and cannon. It was through this connection with the regional classical music scene that he met and hired director and composer David Kraehenbuehl. In the 1980s Alex built an entire sound recording studio in the workshop where Dave composed and transcribed music and worked on the synthesis and programming of music and animation for Alex's ever more sophisticated music machines. Kraehenbuehl observed. "I had no idea, really, what I was getting into. It's all a kind of crazy, fantastic game."[57] The 1980s were a turning point in Alex's development of music and animation and mark an increasing reliance on synthesized music and a turning away from analog systems towards computer generated sound and controls.

CHAPTER 7

IN THE COURT OF THE MOGUL

Not long after purchasing the neighboring farm in 1964 Alex borrowed $10,000 from his cousin Magdalena Brooks to develop it into a large workshop and storage space. He remodeled the old buildings on the site and built new structures to accommodate his needs. This workshop became the hub of many of his creative activities for the next two decades. Most of the artifacts acquired, restored, or created for The House on the Rock collections passed through the workshop. Alex was very proprietary about the activities and creations of the workshop and strictly forbade employees from taking pictures and frowned upon too much talk about the projects under way. In this respect he was no different from other creative entrepreneurs who jealously guard their work. Only a select few dealers and traders he knew were allowed to visit him in the shop. He would occasionally offer a guided tour to an industry VIP, but he carefully controlled what they saw. He would not discuss what he was doing and at times seemed even to deny the existence of the workshop.

All of the music machines that he created or had restored were worked on in the organ restoration and repair department of the shop. An entire theater organ was built there, disassembled, and then transported to The House on the Rock when finished. All of the carousel animals in The House on the Rock collections, including all of those on the Carousel, were restored or created there. It was something of a factory at times employing dozens of workers—a sculptor, painters, organ technicians, an assembly section for chandeliers, and workstations for whatever other projects were underway. The contents of the shop shifted as new collections and materials came in to be stored or transformed into new artifacts. Trucks would arrive daily with loads of building materials, and there was Alex, of course, rolling up in his van often filled with whatever he happened to be collecting at the time—all to be unloaded and stored away—all the raw material of his creativity.

Workshop (early 1970s)

In the 1970s the main workshop consisted of a series connected buildings. The first was the old machine shed from the farm that was remodeled as the main workshop. This was connected to two barn-size structures Alex constructed for the storage of materials and artifacts. The lower shop (structures were built on a gentle slope) area was part of one of these barns and had high ceilings to accommodate huge artifacts. The adjacent high barn-like buildings were filled literally to the rafters with organs, organ pipes and parts, carousel animals, sculptures, buildings materials, architectural salvage, religious statues, stained glass, thousands of decorative moldings that he called "goo gahs," bins full of statuary, band organs, picture frames, and truck loads of chandeliers crammed in floor to ceiling. At the height of Alex's creativity and collecting it was difficult to walk through the warehouses—you had to squeeze sideways and weave your way through caverns of stuff. Often he would come in and ask where such and such an item was. Longer-term employees who had watched the materials arrive or had unloaded them pretty much knew where everything was. Newer people were sent into a panic when he gave them vague directions about where the artifact might be—they often came back empty handed and Alex would have a *petit mal*, raging about all the theft that was going on. In truth, some theft was undoubtedly taking place, but more often the artifact would turn up somewhere in the jumble. Alex eventually acquired two other farms and filled the barns with more carriages, pipe organs and building materials. He was not gathering all this stuff just for the sake of accumulation; he intended to use all of it in his work. He sometimes didn't know exactly how he was going to use the various materials that he acquired, but he knew that sooner or later he would find a use.

In the summertime there were fewer employees working in the shop and Alex often found it a refuge from the activity and demands of The House on the Rock attraction. This was especially true as the attraction grew rapidly and the business and all of the details of the operation became more burdensome. The lower shop was generally a cool place for him to sit; the attraction (with the exception of the small office) was not air-conditioned. Often there were several activities going on in separate parts of the shop: he might visit with the author (sculptor), Jim McKahan (painter), Virginia Reynolds (dollhouse construction and other crafts), and Neil Hanson (band organ construction and restoration). During a typical visit he would sit in his chair, sometimes for hours, watching the work—sometimes sleeping. In the sculpture area, he sat in an old broken-down aluminum plastic-webbed lawn chair that he refused to have repaired even when the webbing became badly frayed and looked like it would collapse under his weight.

He brought along books, magazines or clippings to show me design ideas that he was thinking about; he would occasionally have a book or article he wanted me to look at and I sometimes brought in an art book for him to borrow. Often he would have workers tack up an illustration, picture or drawing on the huge double doors in the lower work area. These doors were covered with bits of picture and paper as high as we could reach. Disgruntled employees also used this space to write or draw insults about Alex in ambiguous or coded form.

One day Alex came in full of himself and declared: "Restoration is that last refuge of he who cannot create." Painter Jim MacKahan lettered this on the door where it remains to this day. It was not that he didn't respect restoration, it was just that we were not in that business here. Surely, antiques and collectibles in his collections were repaired and restored—he was no fool.

Alex in the workshop

His usual schedule was to arrive in the late morning and visit for a while and drop off materials or artifacts. Then he would go to The House on the Rock and visit the sites of new construction, check in at the office, and occasionally meet with business associates. He also found time to tour parts of the attraction. His inspections sometimes resulted in bad consequences for the inattentive or unlucky. His goal was to maintain a unity of vision and high standard for The House on the Rock; he wanted to give his guests the best possible experience and misdirected or burnt-out light bulbs, a bit of trash, or an inattentive employee were not acceptable. He didn't care whose toes got stepped on in the process or who might be gone—there were plenty of hurt toes and empty chairs.

By mid afternoon he was back at the workshop for another visit with the artisans at work there, and then he was back in his van to race home. In spite of his attention to all of the details of the business and his general inability to really delegate, his own perception of his management style was evident when he once told me, "I always felt that I kept a loose hand on the tiller." Maybe that was true for some of the creative staff, but people in many in other parts of the enterprise would not have agreed with this assessment of his methods.

Every day he brought out most of the materials and supplies needed to build or maintain the attraction. In the beginning he drove station wagons and he would trade in every few years. When vans became available he bought a series of larger and larger vehicles with bigger capacity to carry the loads. He often arrived overloaded with material sticking out the back of the open doors nearly dragging on the pavement. When he bought a new van he would arrive and put it through the gas test. He ran the tank nearly empty and marked where the needle was on the gauge, then he would find a "volunteer," give him a gallon can filled with gas, and tell him to drive down the highway until he ran out, record the mileage, put the gallon in and return. He was trying to find out how far he could go when he was running low. His idea of vehicle maintenance was not standard. When a worker said he had to leave early to get his oil changed, Alex said, "You're wasting your money, I never change the oil."

His recycling of old and used things and his economy are legendary; he stopped along the road more than once to pick up a discarded trash can lid or some other treasure. Getting new tools out of him was a test of wills, even for an 89 cent putty knife. But then he would get excited about a project and declare: "I'm going to throw a bushel basket of money at this. I'm going to spend like a drunken sailor." Inconsistent, but then, he was fond of the Emerson quote: "A foolish consistency is the hobgoblin of small minds." In the middle of the cold winter with the shop busy and no money coming in he would jest, "Well I guess Jennie and I are going to have to crank up the old Model T and head for the poor house."

He haunted the cavernous "Diagon Alley" stacks of Paul's Used Bookstore near his Madison home searching for books of interest. He was not an antiquarian collector but occasionally picked up a classic volume he could not resist. He did collect nearly all of the classic works illustrated by Gustav Doré, whose work he respected and enjoyed. The work of Doré was the stuff of romantic inspiration for Alex. He was taken with the Doré-illustrated editions of Coleridge's *Rhyme of the Ancient Mariner*, the romantic *Sword and the Scimitar*, *The Doré Illustrated Bible*, and especially Dante's *Inferno*. The *Inferno* would inspire him his entire life and he returned to it again and again in his initial designs for the Organ Room and late in life in an unrealized dreamy, wistful plan to turn the entire book into a dark ride with animated sculptures. Although he had abandoned religious faith, he treated Biblical characters and stories as literature and was not reluctant to use religious objects and themes in his work. He incorporated religious paintings and sculpture into the attraction, notably in the Mill House with a copy of Matthias Grunewald's *Isenheim Altarpiece* and later in The Music of Yesterday where he created an entire display of Madonnas. After seeing a movie depicting a particularly gruesome crucifixion scene he humphed and said, "Let's do [sculpt] a big crucifixion—I'll show them a crucifixion they won't forget!" He never followed through on this idea.

He seldom bought new books preferring to get a deal at Paul's where he was not afraid to occasionally pay what he considered a lot ($30) for a volume saying, "If you get one good idea out of it you can use, it's very well worth it." He subscribed to a large number of magazines (reportedly over thirty) on a wide range of subjects: specialized collecting, antiques and art, current affairs, news magazines, humor, architecture, sewerage, finance, music, etc. He bought just about every serialized edition of illustrated works on history and culture in the *Time-Life* series.

Alex's musical tastes tended toward the classical. His record collection (hundreds of LPs) was mostly classical leaning, as one would suspect, toward the Romantics, although the collection did sweep through the whole world of classical music into the early twentieth century. His familiarity with this genre is easily traced in the selections he used in the music machines he built (see CHAPTER 6). But his tastes were not exclusively classical. He also appreciated instrumental versions of popular standards that he used in program music filled the House in the early years. The music came from a huge reel-to-reel tape machine that he said could play for eight hours. The collection also contains a good number of recordings of band organs, orchestrions, and circus band music he used to learn about band organs when he was creating his music machines. He was familiar with a wide range of organ music that he collected while building the great theatre organ. He did not care for rock and roll, hated Elvis, and his opinion of John Lennon was, "I don't know what all the fuss is about."

He had a basic grasp of western art and an appreciation of the art of the east. The woodcuts of the fifteenth- and sixteenth-century artist Albrecht Durer, the engravings of Giovanni Piranesi, and the entire architectural and artifact production of Mad King Ludwig were favored by Alex. He had an interest in the work of the fifteenth-century painter Hieronymus Bosch. He never warmed to abstract art although he said he gave Picasso a long try but in the end he just couldn't go there. He had contempt for Jackson Pollock saying, "That Jackson Pollock, he's the worst." He was more of a nineteenth-century man in his tastes and tended to appreciate sculpture more than painting. When a craftsmen embellished one of the creations with one too many pieces of scrollwork (goo-gahs) he would laugh and say, "Ah, there goes Louis the last." The later French kings and the palace at Versailles were especially fascinating to him.

There are countless stories about Alex's treatment of employees, his angry tirades, and summary firings which many times started by his asking, "Did you drive your own car today?" When the employee answered, "Yes," Alex would say, "Well, use it to get out of here." Sometimes the dismissal would be accompanied by angry shouts and insults and after, short summaries of the departed were offered to nobody in particular such as, "He couldn't find his ass with both his hands."

John Korb, The House on the Rock manager in those years, said, "There were a lot of people who got fired who really didn't get fired." He told about an employee who was let go by Alex on Tuesday and on Thursday Alex asked Korb, "Where's so and so?" Korb replied, "Well, you fired him on Tuesday." Jordan replied, "What the hell did I do that for? Get him back." Some "fired" employees were given tasks out of Alex's view and once the storm had passed were reintegrated into the workforce without Alex realizing it.[58] In the middle of the 1980s, with the summer workforce nearing one hundred, Alex had even more trouble keeping track. He had John photograph each employee and keep the pictures in a loose-leaf binder; when somebody got out of line he would come in and go through the book pointing to the offending person and say, "That one, fire that one." Sometimes it even happened.

My observation in the shop was that most of the people he fired deserved to be let go, but nobody deserved the harsh treatment they got from Alex. Many of the jobs were low-skill manual labor and the turnover was high. He was especially irate when employees forgot who owned the place or worked outside the scope of the projects, going off on their own to create their own statement. The second day I worked for him he came in, sat down and said, "You know, we don't want any artists around here." I understood the warning and told him, "You won't get any of that out of me." His policies were not too much different from those enforced at Disney or other commercial creative institutions—we were working under his direction in The House on the Rock style. Don Martin, who worked for Alex for longer than anyone (1956-1989), put it right when he said, "He figured if someone didn't want to work here, he'd find someone else who did." Alex Jordan did not suffer fools gladly.

He did mellow with age, and employees at the end of his life could not believe the stories of his temper tantrums and rudeness from just ten years before. Even in the 1970s he once in a while let his lighter side show through. On one occasion he came to visit the shop as usual in the afternoon where he sat and relaxed in his lawn chair. He got up to leave and I noticed his shoes. I said, "Hey, you've got one black shoe and one brown shoe, what's the deal?" He looked down at his feet and said, "That's OK, I've got pair just like them at home." In those years he would often bring gifts to reward work he liked, sometimes leaving them in employees' cars. The more human side did shine through.

He once told me "You have to hire twelve and fire eleven to get one good one." There were few whom he considered long-term employees but in his mind he was paying people to work for him until he did not need them. It wasn't a regular corporate employment situation; there were no healthcare benefits, retirement, or sick days—if you worked, you got paid, if you didn't, you didn't—and Alex made no promises about the future. Although these seem like harsh conditions, nobody was being forced to work at The House on the Rock, and the pay scale was certainly not attractive—it was obvious that this was a temporary job. Most of his employees were laid off at the end of the season on November first. Some construction and shop personal worked throughout the whole year and a few staff from the attraction itself were carried over during the winter depending on the size of the projects that were underway. Alex never really had any effective shop management so people were left on their own to do their work; he came in every day to see the progress.

Alex never adjusted to the growth of his enterprise and this contributed to the ebb and flow of the chaos of the work environment. His lack of basic people skills played a large part, but also in his mind some part of him remained back in the early 1960s when it was just Don Martin, a few workers and him; he wanted to run the business out of his back pocket. Into the late 1970s employees wrote down the number of hours they had worked under their hand-lettered name in a loose-leaf notebook, no timecards or time clock. Don Martin picked up the book every week and phoned the hours into the accountant. Finally the state stepped in and forced him to keep more formal records and comply with their regulations—he resented this intrusion into his business but also understood he had no choice in the matter.

The lack of structure brought out the best and the worst in workers and The House on the Rock went through cycles of uproar and political intrigue as the pecking order shifted. This was made more complex on the shop side in the winter when additional employees were added to the crowded space. At times, Alex seemed to enjoy and foster the Byzantine politics that swirled around him. Three things were whispered to the newly hired: he has an unpredictable mean streak and heads do roll, he has a dark and shameful past, he is single with no heirs. It was more like a medieval royal court than a place of employment, with court jesters and ambitious sycophants circling and literally following behind him vying to be favored.

Greg Burke tells about his first day: "On my first day we were working on concrete, drilling and beating with a mall, Alex, a large man, said to me, 'I want to hear that mall hit every ten seconds. If you get tired give it to your buddy here.'" He also reflected, "Once you got on his shit list, you were gone. If he liked you, you were in good stead."[59]

If the circumstances of employment were so bizarre, why did people stay? For many it was just a job, either a starter job for those just out of high school or a stopgap for the unemployed. Usually these folks had a short stay; some remained a season or two without any conflict with Alex. There was a succession of skilled artisans who plied their craft for Alex and made significant contributions to The House on the Rock. These skilled artisans often stayed for years and faired a great deal better; they used the experience to hone their skills for future careers: Bob Searles worked with Alex on The Streets of Yesterday and went on to become a well-known porcelain sculptor, John Hovancak designed and built a number of the most loved music machines at The House on the Rock and later became a world-class restorer of antique music machines, painter Jim McKahan went on to teach at the University of Wisconsin. These and many more disciplined their skills—in fact sometimes learned their skills—working with Alex. Generations of workers shifted through.

Jim McKahan, a Vietnam veteran then living in the hills of southwestern Wisconsin, was typical of the artists who wandered into the shop and stayed for a number of years. Jim first came out to The House on the Rock in the late 1950s attending one of the parties Alex was famous for hosting at the House before it was opened to the public. He needed some winter work in 1975 and a friend told him there was work at The House on the Rock workshops saying, "It's a crappy job, but you'll probably last through the winter." The job was stripping the paint off old carousel horses—crappy—and toxic. He let Alex know he had done a little artwork and Alex asked him if he could paint carousel horses like his resident painter Mark Miller. Jim, having nothing to lose, said he could— which was the correct answer. He was put to the test and lead painter Mark Miller helped him through the first horse and he was on his way. The painting method employed at The House on the Rock and introduced by Mark is a dark- to-light system derived from the techniques of the Flemish masters according to Jim. The system achieves a deep luster through the use of alternating glazes and is unique to The House on the Rock; carousel animals were never painted like this before.

Jim recalls, "I had complete artistic freedom but within the scope of the project. My only instruction from Alex was early on when he shuffled in and said, 'All I want from you is when I come out here in the afternoon every day I want to see something that is going to knock my socks off.' And I took that as my guide, I liked that—that's a good way to frame things…I had to dazzle him with my footwork, and the more I did of it I started getting bored, and that actually increased my imagination because I tried to always go beyond…." It was typical that Alex, once he trusted an artist, gave them freedom with the project and sometimes went a long time without offering direction. Jim further reflected on the experience echoing other artists who worked for Alex when he said, "There was the professional side—you had to deliver something every day, some days are better than others but it taught you discipline…it was a good training ground because I had relative freedom, and it gave you confidence in your ability. He would just hand me the ball and I had to run with it."[60]

I showed up at The House on the Rock workshop in August of 1977. I was not hired by Alex, but by the shop manager. There was already a sculptor on staff, Ted Lang, who had made many contributions to the carousel and other projects. Ted was on vacation and I never knew whether I was hired as an additional sculptor or to replace Ted who, it turned out, did not know that he was moving on. The manager showed me the workspace and the carousel horses undergoing repair and then left. Jim McKahan came down and told me to keep my head down because Jordan was an unpredictable and moody guy and people get fired. I thought, "Oh, great, I don't know what I'm supposed to do and there's this lunatic on his way here." I saw that one of the horses had a leg missing so I sort of carved one out of a piece of two-by-four. Late in the morning Jordan blew in with a noisy ruckus trailed by the shop manager who seemed to be explaining why he had hired somebody without telling him. The manager took a mild defensive posture explaining that I had carved this leg. Alex looked at it and said, "All right, nice, but let's see what this guy can do. I've got this fiberglass lion over here [a carousel figure] I want you to make some changes to it—I want it to be rampant, you know what I mean?" I said, "Yeah, I know what you mean." And then he breezed out.

I recognized this as the Jordan test. For Alex, first impressions were everything. This was a first impression that was going to take until the next day about 11 a.m. to finish. And I had the feeling that like Jane Austen's Mr. Darcy, Alex might well say, "My feelings are not puffed about with every attempt to move them. My temper would perhaps be called resentful. My good opinion once lost, is lost forever."[61] I was right about all that.

I hauled the lion into the open space of the crowded workshop and found a reciprocating saw and cut off the legs. I turned it over on its side and cut into the head through the thick mane. I was now standing on the lion that was pounding up and down on the concrete making quite a racket as the dull blade hacked its way through. Just as the head came flying off skidding across the floor Alex appeared. He looked at the scene before him and said in a sort of low voice, "You know what you're doing, don't you?" "Yeah," was all I said, and he was gone. The rest of the afternoon and the next morning workers in the shop seemed to be avoiding coming down to the lower level where I was working, and I got the feeling that I was sitting on some sort of time bomb that was about to go off. I got the lion all back together and in a rampant pose by the time Alex re-appeared the next day and he was pleased. "Well I see we've got a real artist working for us now," is what he said. The first impression was over, but more importantly I had learned what was going on. There were two shows here: that one across the road at the attraction where the tourists were paying for the experience, and the show here where I had to entertain him every day.

Over the next years he presented one challenge after another as he ticked through a list of carousel animals he wanted built. Every day he came in and sat in his chair as I worked, and I probed for conversation with this man of few words. To find things to talk about I brought in books and magazines with pictures and articles of interest to him. He brought his notebooks and showed me some of his plans for the future. Some days he would sit watching the work for hours, making a few comments, looking at books or magazines, or sleeping. He often said it was the best place in the whole institution and that he wanted to retire and sit and watch me work [Oh, no!]. Through our brief conversations I gradually began to understand the methods he used and his system of display.

He sometimes held court in the workshop as I worked and the occasional collector or associate would visit; I always listened carefully to try to learn more. Through all the ups and downs Alex allowed me, and Jim, a great degree of artistic freedom sometimes giving minimal or no direction within the scope of the project. He was grateful and said so, showing up with gifts, usually bottles of booze left in the car. He insisted that I should keep a bottle on the job "for snakebite," which I never did. Through the many small and large projects we were involved in together, we never had a cross word. Like the other artists who worked for Alex, I have always been grateful for the opportunity to learn and to be challenged, and I join their voices in saying that the experience was unique and irreplaceable.

Alex learned the value of a dollar from his parents and remembered well the difficulties of the Depression of the 1930s. His economy was legendary as he kept track of every expense and squeezed every penny. The pay was low but as Greg Burke put it, "Money for himself didn't matter. The reason why he scrutinized things like light bulbs or toilet paper was so he could build other projects…also for Iowa County, his wages weren't bad."[62] Alex believed (in a somewhat facile creed for a wealthy man) "A man is not poor because he has nothing, but because he does nothing."

For those working on the creative side, it was just so darned interesting to come in every day—sometimes just to see what was going to happen. Alex was always planning projects and coming up with ideas that were challenging. Artisans who understood the facts of life about employment in the arts knew that there were very few places they could get paid for working on creative projects like those underway in the workshops. In addition, it was seductive to be part of the enormous schemes.

Some employees stayed in admiration of Alex's creativity, looking up to him as a genius, even a father figure. One day he came walking into the shop reading a magazine article as he walked. I asked him what it was and he replied chuckling, "Oh nothing, I'm just a genius again." The all-too-human Alex quietly enjoyed this adulation and was not above playing to his fans.

There were those who considered the future beyond their aging boss who, after all, had no heirs, or so they thought. Some hoped for the day when the gossip would hold true and they would be secure Iowa County employees in a post-Alex era—he was rumored to have left The House on the Rock to Iowa County.[63] There were many who continued to work for Alex simply because they found ways to live within the environment, found him fascinating, intriguing and sometimes entertaining, and the work acceptable. Whatever their motivations were, they gathered around him and formed a staff that was loyal to him and to The House on the Rock. Don Martin remembered him this way: "He was a nice guy to work for, there were those who wouldn't agree…we did get along. I knew when to walk away. You learned about his good days and his bad days."[64]

In the fall of 1977 a disgruntled ex-employee filed a sixty-point complaint with Occupational Health and Safety Administration (OSHA) that included the whole attraction and the workshops. Inspectors came and combed through The House on the Rock and the workshops and listed a total of ten violations of the electrical code and assessed a fine of $270.[65] Alex corrected the problems one by one including the installation of an employee fire escape from the top of The House on the Rock—a requirement not listed in the original complaint but required under new OSHA regulations. Alex contracted engineer Rolf Killingstad who designed a structure that satisfied the concerns of the federal agency. Alex was embarrassed by the negative press coverage that the OSHA citations generated. However, none of this affected attendance that continued to rise.

More serious accusations striking at the very heart of the business became public in 1978 when the Wisconsin Department of Justice responded to complaints from disaffected ex-employees. Over the years the P.T. Barnum showman part of Alex Jordan had gotten a little out of hand. He began (or others had in his name) to make claims about his displays that were not accurate. For example, he claimed The Franz Josef music machine was actually built in Germany to celebrate the fiftieth anniversary of the monarch's reign— the case was built by a local contractor and the musical components of the machine were built in The House on the Rock workshops. The advertising claimed that an apparent elephant tusk carving was the "Tusk of Ranchipur" created by an unknown Punjab carver—it is plastic and was put together by a local craftsman. In addition, a few nineteenth-century dates were inserted here and there. A picture book that Alex sold to the public he called "The Brochure" offered a colorful guided tour of the attraction in words and photos. In the early 1960s when Howard Mead, editor of the magazine *Wisconsin Tales and Trails,* wrote a descriptive and complimentary article about The House on the Rock in his magazine, Alex used it as the foundation of his picture book that served the attraction in the 1960s. In the early 1970s Alex produced his own promotional picture book written under his direction. The claims became exaggerated and the text turned from favorable reporting to purple prose—Alex could never resist a little mischief.

Attorney General Bronson La Follette was not amused and initiated a six-month investigation (1978) under the direction Assistant Attorney General Bruce Craig. Investigators toured The House on the Rock, taking photographs of exhibit labels and suspicious displays. They traveled to California to research attractions like Disneyland and Knott's Berry Farm. At one point the researchers intimated that they thought the attraction should be shut down.[66] At the end of his investigation Craig said that, "It was difficult for us to decide whether Jordan, who has clearly put a lot of time and money into the displays, set out to deliberately lie to the public or whether he was just out to flavor things."

A front-page story in *The Capital Times* in August of 1978 reported: "The theory that too much enthusiasm and license was used in describing some of the displays is shared by Jordan as well. He said it was a matter of 'a little too much show biz—I started it, and others just followed, each adding on a little more, to hype House on the Rock displays.' Jordan sadly admitted that the false advertising wasn't necessary—the House itself and the displays are good enough to stand on their own, without any verbal embellishments."[67]

The Department of Justice obtained a stipulation judgment that Alex signed. I asked him about all this and he said: "They made me sign a paper that said I didn't do anything wrong—but I wouldn't do it again." Others in the workshop tried to make light of the situation by telling him they were insulted that they had not been named un-indicted co-conspirators.

But all that was just bravado in front of the boys. Alex was very worried and upset by all of this and said that Jennie was also saddened. There would be no more mislabeling or false advertising in the future of The House on the Rock, and his souvenir picture book was cleaned up too. Craig summed it up this way: "I think what Jordan decided somewhere along the line was that what he was doing out there was impressive enough that it wasn't necessary to gild the lily. Show business people are used to puffing things up. Rather than being a crook, he was just someone who got carried away."[68] Attendance did not drop off because of this. More people came; some showed up with the newspaper clippings in hand looking for the now infamous "Tusk of Ranchipur" and other artifacts.

One of the ideas Alex returned to throughout the years was his great animated clock. There are a number of drawings in his notebooks and it was on his mind until the end of his life. This was to be a huge outdoor clock (a building really) in the tradition of European tower clocks with animated figures that came out on the hour, and bells and music. He talked about it often. One day while I was working in the shop Alex was sitting quietly in his usual chair and he said, "You know what we're going to do? We're going to build that clock." Then he took out his weathered notebook and proceeded to describe the clock and the procession of mythical, religious, and historical figures and the bells and the music, and then he said, "You know what's going to happen at the end? A door is going to open and Attorney General Bronson La Follette will come out bare-assed followed by the devil jabbing him with a pitchfork and sending him right to hell!" We never built it.

CHAPTER 8

"A WONDER, NOTHING LESS"

In the early 1970s as he made progress on The Streets of Yesterday, Alex started to think more seriously about another project he had in mind—a carousel. Not just any carousel would do, it had to be the grandest imaginable. This carousel came to overshadow everything else in the attraction, except the House. Doug Finley, who functioned as personnel manager in Alex's last years, put it accurately when he instructed new Carousel workers, "Visitors who come here only know two things: there's a House up on that rock and there's a carousel."[69]

Though he was reluctant to travel, he visited both Disneyland and Knott's Berry Farm in California to inspect and ride their carousels. He began to make drawings and research merry-go-rounds and gradually started to acquire a few carousel horses. At first, he bought reproductions and sent them to a studio in Chicago to have them painted; eventually he got in contact with carousel dealers and started collecting in earnest. The carousel animals (primarily horses) came to workshops by the truckload in various conditions from all over the United States, and some from Europe and Mexico. Many were found rotting away in barns, abandoned relics of an age gone by. Collectors were just beginning to appreciate the skill of the carvers who produced these works and soon carousel animals became highly collectible. Alex said he thought that he was running just ahead of the collectors who would soon drive the price out of reach.

The carousel animals arrived with coats and coats of paint on them and many were broken or had pieces missing. Alex expanded the workshops to accommodate this new massive project and hired four painters, a varying number of paint strippers and repair people, and a sculptor to work on just the animals for the carousel. What emerged from this effort, led by artists Mark Miller and Jim McKahan, was a new style of painted carousel animal unique to The House on the Rock. The animals were painted in lustrous deep tones and not the garish colors usually associated with carousels (see Chapter 7). All of the work coming out of the workshops served the vision of Alex Jordan and was not signed by the craftspeople. The artisans understood the rules; this is standard policy in the industry, but a few occasionally left their marks in the designs on the figures or in obscure places on the piece—at their own peril. Greg Burke, remembered, "To my knowledge Alex never came out and said, 'this is my design" about any piece…he didn't want to take credit for everything."[70] In the end there were only two pieces in the whole collection that he insisted on having signed by the artist. When the first video about the attraction was produced he didn't like it and wanted it changed. He thought it said "Alex Jordan" too many times, "This is everybody's," he said.[71]

It did not take Alex long to get back on his feet after his brush with death in his 1972 car accident. He found new creative energy and began a decade of rapid building and diverse projects. First he constructed a building with roofs cascading down the hillside. He thought that this would be the Organ Building. He described how the organ would be located way down at the bottom of the hill, which formed a naturally sloping theater. He began construction on the organ chamber that was to contain all of the pipes next to the stage. Then he built the Carousel Building and finally the Inferno Building. As late as the middle 1970s, these buildings were mostly empty, but he had been hard at work designing, collecting, and building the contents.

Empty Doll Carousels building (originally the Organ Room)

A crew of welders, electricians, and laborers led by Tom Every worked on the mechanism and framework of the carousel starting with parts that came from an early twentieth-century carousel manufactured by Gustav Dentzel discovered by antiques dealer Bill Edwards while scouting for antiques in Michigan. The carousel was complete, including fifty-two rare, hand-carved carousel animals. After they installed the carousel mechanism, welders added additional outer rows, re-engineered the ring gear and installed a powerful electric motor. Since their engineering was intuitive, there was the tendency to overbuild everything; they discovered that the original mechanism would not sustain the weight of the additional outer rows so Tom Every installed 18 truck wheels along the outside edge. Alex always joked about this, calling the carousel "his eighteen wheeler."

Although he had amassed a large collection of wooden carousel animals, he was not satisfied. He wanted his carousel to be unique in every way and the usual wooden animals from carousels of the past would not do. In typical Jordan fashion, he pushed the idea of a carousel beyond anything seen before. He imagined creatures more fantastic than on any existing carousel; he began to buy fiberglass carousel reproductions and statues of all kinds and instructed his sculptors, first Ted Lang and then me, to combine these into exotic creatures—centaurs, dragons, and creations too improbable to categorize. For the crown of the Carousel, his designs included a series of peacocks built in the workshops.

The lighting is all Alex's design; he used chandeliers he collected and designed new ones for the Carousel—in the end there would be 182 chandeliers in all. Workmen spent months assembling the Jordan chandeliers; meanwhile, the non-hanging lighting was built (Don Martin and his crew worked on this) and installed, bringing the total number of lights on the carousel to 20,000. Alex was always ready to recite all of the statistics and all of the numbers having to do with the Carousel.

Alex left behind hundreds of drawings and notes that he made between 1965 and 1988. The collection of drawings includes those from the 1970s when he was thinking about and building the great carousel. His creative process generally involved three kinds of drawings. First, he occasionally hired artists to render his concepts in great detail—this was the case for The

Infinity Room, the Jim McKahan drawings for the Organ Room, and the Terry English Circus Room sketches—but for the Carousel he did all the conceptual drawings himself. The second kind of drawing comes from his notebooks. Alex had peculiar sleep habits, sleeping from early evening until 10 p.m. or so, and then reading and drawing until 3 or 4 a.m., and then sleeping again. Most of the drawings from the notebooks were done as he sat alone in the middle of the night planning and dreaming of his creations. The drawings were often labeled with descriptive notes, they were seldom greatly detailed and did not serve as plans but rather as part of his thought process. Third, Alex made field sketches on whatever was lying around to give direction to his workers—these were mostly discarded and only a few survive.

Alex Jordan drawing of the Carousel

Alex always used 5½ x 9 inch paper for his notebook drawings and fabricated the books by stapling several sheets together and then eventually taping the stapled sections together with cellophane tape, making them a size that he could easily stuff in his jacket pocket. The notebooks were a memory aid and a way for him to visualize his thought process; they became yellowed, dog eared, and coffee stained as time went on. Some of the drawings closely represent the finished product, but that was seldom true.

The drawings were the beginning of, or the clarification of, the process—a starting point. These were his points of departure but he did refer back to them as he went along to track his process and progress.

For more than ten years Alex collected decorative elements he thought would be useful for his work on the Carousel. He now brought these out of storage and designed a typical section of the Carousel decoration. The drawings show only a sketchy sense of the effect he was after; it was in the hands-on work that the whole thing came to life. He had workers use the elements to build prototypes. He would tell them what he wanted, leave for the day, come back the next day, make additions or changes or throw the whole thing out and start over, come back the next day and so on until he was satisfied. Once one component was decided, artisans repeated the unit dozens or hundreds of times around the carousel. This went on for years.

While this was going on, he was also directing the creation of the figures for the carousel in The House on the Rock workshops. There are four kinds of figure on the carousel: First, there are hand-carved wooden carousel animals Alex collected from the U.S., Mexico, and Europe; these were restored to their original condition and painted in The House on the Rock style.[72] Some of these works made it on to the Carousel and the remainder, hundreds of hand-carved carousel animals (most of them horses), are hanging on the walls floor-to-ceiling in the Carousel room and in the adjoining Doll Carousels. Second, are fiberglass castings of collectible hand-carved carousel animals Alex purchased, these were also painted in the workshops. Third, he asked his sculptor to combine parts of fiberglass animals to create new creatures of his imagination, such as centaurs, dragons, mermaids, armored centaurs, armored mermaids, and creatures beyond description. Fourth, there are a number of original creations built in the workshop from scratch to his order and installed on the carousel.

It was an organic process—one thing leading to another, one day leading to another with Alex's shifting and changing vision. The building of the Carousel was conducted against the background of economy of time and materials. It got bigger—it was Alex after all—and in the final design became too big for the building; he had to bump out a section of the wall high up to allow the crown of the carousel to clear the building. He quipped, "You can never make a building too big."[73] The process was a dynamic interaction between Alex and his craftspeople, filled with serendipity and happy accidents as well as Alex's vision and the design tradition of The House on the Rock.

The Carousel under construction

Gradually, under Alex's direction, it all came together: the painting, sculpture, lighting and all of his collected and created figures. During the decade that had passed he had directed the building of a wide variety of creations inspired by his broad imagination, making this carousel unlike any other. Now that it was time to install the animals, he had an enormous number of carousel animals to choose from; so many exotics, in fact, that he began to notice that he had not put any horses on the Carousel—a total of 269 creatures and no horses. He was proud of this fact, thinking that it contributed to making the carousel all the more unique.

The Carousel in preparation

As if the Carousel weren't enough, he installed three giant steam tractors along the wall on one side of the room, furnishing them with carnival-like canopies and giving them names with a touch of humor: Firefly, Snowflake, and Buttercup. On a wall adjacent to the carousel he constructed a three-story music machine including enormous copper cheese vats used as drums. Visitors exiting the room passed under this machine and through a large Devil's head to enter the Organ Room. Finally he placed The Gebrueder Bruder band organ next to the Carousel. The Carousel opened in the spring of 1981 to general acclaim and has been a central attraction at The House on the Rock ever since. It is almost beyond description and is, as Alex was fond of saying, "A wonder, nothing less." There was plenty of wonder and plenty to wonder about. A few years after the Carousel opened to the public, Alex acquired a large number of female mannequins. He had them delivered to the shop and instructed his craftspeople to enhance their breasts and add wings and scanty gowns, always leaving the enhanced breasts exposed. He then covered the ceiling of the Carousel Room with them. Some guests were offended while others just snickered, but many thought he had finally slipped over the edge and fallen into the land of kitsch. The bad boy was still alive and needed to poke everyone in the ribs, no matter what they thought.

The finished Carousel

There is a twisting of the idea of a carousel in this Alex Jordan creation. Carousels are always thought of as places of fun—happy places where children smile and adults can briefly be children again. The House on the Rock Carousel is not an amusement park ride. Guests are never allowed on the Carousel, defying the very definition of a Carousel as a Merry-go-Round. Alex explained this using aesthetic reasons—he said that ordinary carousels had to limit the design of the animals, carefully eliminating sharp edges, hard to mount rides, and images that might be problematic for children. He did not want his imagination limited to what had previously been done with carousel design, and then there were all those liability concerns. Alex did not much care for children, whom he considered threats to his displays, climbing and touching as he thought they were likely to do. There is in the oral history of The House on the Rock more than one story related by employees about children running through the complex saying that an old man was chasing them. Outside of the attraction he was more tolerant of younger folks. Still, if the goal had been amusement pleasure, concerns about sharp edges or child-inappropriate designs could have been addressed—that was not the goal.

Alex did not hide himself in his creations but unselfconsciously exposed himself in them. The carousel that can't be ridden is an object not of amusement park pleasure but an object of desire. There is a deeper side here but not sinister, more childlike, not a phantom—not quite. He said that the Carousel was for the "visual pleasure of the general public."[74] Each object, each figure more exotic than the next in a chorus of color and sound that transports the viewer into the deeper realm of desire and the unreachable object which Alex withholds and controls. Love and desire my carousel—love and desire me—but don't come close. In the years of life remaining to him, Alex often sat there alone, anonymously in the shadows enjoying his creation and watching guests' eyes open wide with wonder and desire, mouths agape as they entered the room. The carousel figures whirling by in a blur of color do not fit into any unified thematic category but are a collage of images beyond the logic of time and space, referring as they do to an amalgam of myths and romantic tales and dreamy figures from the underworld of Alex's imagination.

Chapter 9

Inferno

When the gigantic Inferno building, half of a football field long, began to sprawl down the hillside next to the Carousel, Alex saw the enormity of the project. He had filled his notebooks with lists and sketches of ideas he had been working on, and these started to come together in a new form.

Other than Alex Jordan, the person most responsible for the design and execution of the Organ Room was Tom Every. When Every first visited The House on the Rock during the 1960s he recalled, "It was like walking into a heavenly happening to see all that, because I could identify with the sensitivity of The House on the Rock."[75] He had heard of Alex Jordan but had not met him, although his father took him to the fights in Madison in the 1940s where he had seen Alex box. Tom contacted Alex in the late 1960s asking about buying his sleek sixteen-cylinder, custom car to no avail—by then Alex no longer owned the car.

From an early age Tom Every was a collector and trader; he owned an industrial salvage company, Wisconsin By-Products (later doing business as Eveco International) that specialized in large-scale industrial salvage. During his career the company was responsible for the salvage of many industrial and commercial sites in the upper Midwest. Tom was unique in this business because he found aesthetic value in many of the industrial machines and architectural components he was being asked to tear down. He did not scrap pieces that he felt had some "spirit" in them but rather set them aside. This nascent sense of form would later inspire him to become a prominent sculptor in his own right. When he finally met Alex Jordan he found a kindred spirit, though the meeting took place under curious circumstances.

While he was hospitalized recuperating from the December 1972 car collision with a horse that almost cost him his life, Alex's sometimes friend Sid Boyum showed him a newspaper ad run by Every offering used whiskey barrels for sale. Sid called the number and Tom Every showed up at the hospital. Right then and there Alex bought 2000 oak whiskey barrels from him. This was the beginning of their stormy, but productive, friendship. When Alex returned home from the hospital he was weakened and depressed, according to Tom, and could only walk a few feet before he needed to rest. Tom Every often visited him at his home, usually late at night (they were both night owls) and they would sit and look at illustrated books, listen to music, and talk about The House on the Rock. Tom remembers these times with fondness: "All of those hours and hours that I sat with him and looked at books and stuff, it was a good fellowship, and I can't remember a single time we didn't have a good time...I have nothing but respect for Alex because he was focused on what he was doing and all the fellowships were honest...we were like a couple of friends."[76] But the dark side was there in the background—antique dealer Bill Edwards advised Tom to stay away from Jordan, saying he was paranoid. Sid Boyum was not comfortable with Tom's presence. One day Tom came to visit and Alex asked, "What's your game? Do you want The House on the Rock? Well you can have The House on the Rock—you take The House on the Rock and do what you want to do out there!"[77]

Whatever the complex motivations were, they would go on to make wonderful things; during the next few years, Tom expended so much effort for Alex and The House on the Rock and seemed to come so close to Alex that many employees took for granted that he would have some permanent place in the future of the company—maybe even beyond Alex's life. These events played with Every's mind and the minds of some employees who thought of him as the heir apparent. He showed up at The House on the Rock on Sunday afternoons decked out in cravat and sliver-topped cane and gave private tours of the unfinished Organ Room. Alex knew about this and said nothing.

Early in their relationship Alex turned to Tom and said, "There is a great artist in you, and he's struggling to get out." Every began creating fantasy sculptures and machines of his own at his Madison home. His method of working was to gather from his salvage a variety of unrelated components (found objects) and weld them together creating new forms. Part of his aesthetic is not to change any of the components that he uses because he believes the objects contain something of the people who used or made them, as if they are animated by their contact with people. This magical theory would serve Tom later when he wandered off into his own work and became a world-renowned visionary sculptor under the name of Dr. Evermor.[78]

Tom's work with Alex at The House on the Rock served him as a training ground and an exploration of artistic possibility for work to come. Now, in his shop he worked on a large piece combining a variety of found objects and created *The Epicurean,* a fantasy machine that doubles as a backyard barbeque. When he was finished, he invited Alex over to his house to have the first hamburger cooked on the grill. Alex was impressed with *The Epicurean* and sat there eating his burger and not saying much. Tom finally asked him what he thought, and he said, "I can't improve on it."

Later Alex told Tom he wanted *The Epicurean* at The House on the Rock and may even have offered Tom a food concession in what was then called the Inferno Room.[79] Tom talked about designing tables to be scattered along the terraces that were being built in the room and the installation of *The Epicurean* at the lower end of the building where a theater organ would entertain guests as they dined.

Alex was still troubled by the projects that were now underway: the Carousel and The Inferno Room. He studied and read all he could about carousels and theater organs, subscribed to professional journals and enthusiasts' magazines. In 1975, Alex and Tom embarked on one of three trips they would make to California. Alex did not like to travel and usually wanted to get home the same day but for *these* trips they stayed a few days. They visited Knott's Berry Farm, an amusement park that grew up around a family berry farm and restaurant. The ghost town and park were built so that the people waiting in line for dinner had something to do to distract them—eventually the park became more important than the restaurant. Jordan and Every walked through the ghost town and looked at the rides but Alex was most interested in the recently installed carousel. They both rode it and studied and discussed the construction. They also visited Disneyland where again Alex's main interest was the carousel, which they looked at carefully and also rode.

The second trip to California was to visit the Nethercutt Museum in Sylmar, California. The museum, known as the Tower of Beauty, is the collection of J.B. Nethercutt whose fortune came from the Merle Norman Cosmetics Company founded by his aunt. The Tower contains the Nethercutt collection of restored antique cars as well as a prized collection of dolls. The Music Room also features a Wurlitzer pipe organ that rises out of the floor and a Louis XV style dining room, as well as the Nethercutt world-class collection of orchestrions, reproducing pianos, music boxes, and nickelodeons. Alex took all of this in, searching for ways to develop his own collection and continue designs for the Organ Room.

The third trip was supposed to be arranged by Tom Every, but he didn't get all the details right. The purpose of the trip was to visit manufacturers of fiberglass carousel animals. When they landed at the airport in San Francisco Tom realized that he had not made arrangements for a rental car. To complicate matters neither of them had a credit card. So Tom led the way from one rental agency desk to the next, Tom dressed in his suit and Alex trailing behind shuffling along in his baggy corduroy pants, sloppy shirt, and "Hush Puppy" shoes. The rental agencies turned them down one after another, and Alex started to get madder and madder until Tom took him over to the waiting area and told him to "wait here." Tom produced a House on the Rock brochure which had a portrait of Alex in it and went back over to one of the desks and said: "I'm in a lot of trouble, I was supposed to make the car arrangements and now he told me point blank, 'Buy the sonofabitchen car, I got enough cash in my pocket!' Every continues, "I told the lady that he is a little bit eccentric and a little bit different and I don't know if he will hit me over the head, but he was not happy with me not booking that car ahead of time, and here is a picture of him in the brochure and he has told me to buy the car. I think that the lady took pity on me and gave me the car with no cash down or anything, just my signature."

In 1975 Tom and Eleanor Every joined Alex on an excursion to Florida. They spent a few days and visited two sites. First they went to Ten Oaks, the Brown Estate in Clearwater; the estate had extensive landscaped gardens and a large Italian-style villa. Many artifacts were up for sale—Alex was interested in the pipe organ, Tom purchased a gold leaf, square grand piano, and they inspected a large chime tower at the water's edge (which reportedly the neighbors hated). Tom was fascinated by the chimes and thought that Alex should buy them for The House on the Rock, but Alex was not so sure. Two weeks later after they had returned to Madison, Alex called Tom and told him he had bought the chimes. Tom eventually installed them in the new chime tower that he built for them in the Organ Building.

The second site they visited was the Ringling Museum in Sarasota, which includes the Ringling art collection, the CA d'Zan (an Italian villa on Sarasota Bay), and the Ringling Circus Museum which houses the circus memorabilia collected by John and Mabel Ringling. Their tour of the museum was uneventful. Next they went on the guided tour of the Ringling home. It was a hot and sticky Florida day and Alex had his checkered long-sleeved shirt slung over his shoulder, long oversized tee shirt hanging over his ample frame, the usual corduroy pants and brown "Hush Puppy" shoes.

He was sweating profusely and all the people were backed up in the hallway next to the marble bathroom. Alex couldn't see and he lost his patience; he started elbowing his way up to the front, wheedling through the crowd saying: "I'm a plumber from Wisconsin and I got to get in there to see these pipes." They all parted and he got in to see the pipes. It was not the first, or last, time he impersonated a plumber. These were good times for Tom and Eleanor and for Alex. Alex was on the verge of his most creative work. For Tom there was a lot of hard work ahead, a lot of ups and downs, and when he was done with The House on the Rock and Alex Jordan he would feel he had lost everything— whether this was true or not, he certainly had gained a great deal—but that was still some time off.[80]

Alex explained his travel experience to a reporter: "When I go somewhere away from here it's strictly business, no pleasure...Last week I was in Florida for a few days looking for something. When I came back somebody asked me how the weather was. I said I didn't notice the weather. I mean, damn it, when I go looking for something, that's what's on my mind! Not the damn weather."[81]

The idea of the Organ Room gradually took shape in Alex's mind while he was working on The Streets of Yesterday and his music machines. He continued to refer in his drawings to The Wayfarer's Chapel, that he sketched in at the exit of the Carousel Room—he even mentioned it to a reporter. When Bill Edwards began to find a variety of religious statues, stained glass, and church architectural embellishments Alex bought everything Edwards could find for him. His vision began to clarify when he realized that the building he had built for the theatre organ was not going to be large enough to house everything he was considering for the room. His vision shifted and was transformed into the Inferno Room idea taken from Dante's *Divine Comedy*. The inspiration came from the illustrations of Dante's works by the nineteenth-century engraver Gustav Doré. Alex collected leather-bound editions of Doré illustrations; he pored over these books and returned to them for inspiration time and time again, not only for the Inferno Room project but also for the Carousel and other projects.

Doré Illustration of a scene from Dante's *Inferno*

In his descriptions of The Inferno Room he planned a walking tour of the Doré *Inferno* illustrations brought to life as sculptures. The vision was a dark and wandering journey through the circles of hell amid animated sculptures of the damned. This he wanted to combine with the lugubrious sounds of the great theatre organ. Part of the vision was the movement of the guests as they made their way along the paths; he considered this movement of the visitors to be an essential part of the design. His architectural inspiration for the room came from an eighteenth-century Italian architect/artist, Giovanni Battista Piranesi, who created prints of grand imaginary interiors. Alex was especially taken with a series of Piranesi etchings known as the *Carceri d'invenzione* (Imaginary Prisons) depicting huge underground cave-like spaces filled with stairways, columns, towers, architectural vaulting, and enormous machinery. This aesthetic of Doré, Dante, and Piranesi he envisioned against the background of his love for the works of the fifteenth and sixteenth-century painter Hieronymus Bosch whose terrible and glorious visions fascinated him.

Piranesi engraving of "Imaginary Prisons"

Dante's *Inferno* is set in the darkness of the underworld and it is ironic that today's room is often described by guests as being underground in a cave or in a basement; the building spans a hillside and on the lower end is actually more than five stories high. Although he changed his mind about the concept of the Inferno Room, Alex stuck to his dark vision and followed his own advice to "make it mysterious." In the fall of 1978, it was still the Inferno Room and he ordered the author to build as the entrance a twenty-foot high Devil's head based on an illustration from an unidentified book he brought in. This was one of the few times he consented to have me make a model first. He usually thought models were a waste of time. Visitors still pass through this portal, but they do not enter the Inferno Room; they enter a room transformed into what he now called the Organ Room. Alex was very much pleased when the first child to approach the Devil's Head stopped dead, looked up, and then, frightened, turned around and ran back to his parents saying he didn't want to go through.

Devil's Head

One end of the enormous building was left open during construction so that trucks and a crane could drive right in. The hillside terrain was not altered much; concrete retaining walls were poured to define the terraces, winding pathways, and descending floor levels. The immense chandelier and grand artifacts inspired by Piranesi remained, but the Dante sculptures and *Inferno* theme faded away; the only vestige of the *Inferno* are the looming statues peering down from the dark recesses of the room.

Alex supervising the Organ Room construction

The religious statues were rebuilt along secular themes. When work began on the remodeling of the statues Alex told me, "My father would not have approved of this." But the work continued and the figures were resculpted and sent to the paint room where they were finished. The shop filled up with figures staring out (some with glass eyes). They stood there for a few weeks. Finally, Alex had somebody get some garbage bags and cover their heads. Jim McKahan suggested that all those eyes looking out at him made Alex uncomfortable.

The theme for the room was now the grand theater organ his staff was constructing. The theater organ project had been underway since the late 1960s and Alex envisioned it as the largest organ in the world. It started like all his other projects: first he bought a theater organ that became available, then a few parts here and there, then another organ, and it grew from there. The House on the Rock theater organ is made up of the remains of many smaller theater and church organs Alex combined into one grand super organ. Alex's collection of theater organs and parts of organs filled his warehouses with pipes and components; a staff of organ builders led by organ-specialist Dave Junchen spent many months on the project. The main organ, along with its roll-playing mechanism, was assembled and tested in the workshop where Alex enjoyed listening to powerful renditions of the classics including "The 1812 Overture" and occasionally his mother's favorite song, "The Rosary" by Ethelbert Nevin. Neighbors in the surrounding valleys reported hearing strange musical sounds on summer evenings. Eventually the organ was taken apart and moved from the workshop to the Organ Room.

The old steam water works from the Nichols Pumping Station in the city of Madison became available for salvage, and Tom Every removed it and hauled it out to The House on the Rock. He poured the footings and supports and lifted the sixty-ton pump into place. In Alex's vision, the machine would dominate the room as the giant wheel slowly turned and a walking beam (added later) pumped up and down. Tom soon added a second smaller pump from the University of Wisconsin and somewhere along the line the whole idea of the space began to change. The Inferno Room concept was eclipsed by a new vision—a magical industrial fantasy—a montage of machinery and the detritus of manufacturing plants, converted religious statues, sculptures, a tremendous chandelier, a number of Alex's collections, giant clocks, and above and through it all the giant theater organ.

The giant pump in place in the empty Organ Room

At times the Organ Room seemed to have turned into a giant sandbox for both Alex and Tom. These were two strong egos and there was a great deal of back and forth and sometimes heated discussion about how to proceed; in the end, Alex was in charge and all of it came about under his direction. The identity of the salvaged industrial artifacts in the room reads like the history of upper Midwest manufacturing. The construction scene was chaotic. There were daily deliveries of organ parts for the grand organ, brew kettles from defunct breweries, odds and ends of businesses that were updating or selling out. Copper tanks came in from around the state; the giant tanks from Horlick's Malted Milk factory were originally imported from England are three-eights-inch thick. Enormous brew kettles from the Kingsbury Brewery and tanks from the People's Brewery in Oshkosh found homes along the dark walkways of the Organ Room along with motors from Gisholt Company in Madison, all of them swallowed up by the massive room. The list of salvaged materials goes on and on, all of it headed for the scrap heap but here granted new life as part of this fantasy assemblage. All the copper vats were ground, polished and sealed and thousands of bricks were laid as floor pavement. In keeping with his vision derived from Piranesi, Alex had Tom and his crew of welders build a series of arching bridges, in Alex's words, "to bring the whole room together." Alex also ordered sculptures from his workshops and creations by his artisans, and over the course of time the mysterious and inspired room took shape.

In the center, a giant chandelier ("World's Largest") lights the winding pathway; this alone is an engineering marvel and the source of heated arguments between Alex and Tom. Their tempestuous relationship would have them disgusted and shouting at each other one day and walking into the room arm in arm the next. Alex designed an office for his own use to be built into the center of the chandelier where he thought that he would be able to hide away (this was never built). Secret spaces to which he could escape, or fantasize escape, and from which he could watch his creations and visitors were a reoccurring feature of Alex's thoughts: the hidden room in the fireplace in the Mill House that was advertised in the literature in the 1970s but never built, a small private office tucked away above The Music of Yesterday, and now an office in the grand chandelier. These plans are the introvert's desire to be apart from people but still take pleasure in public reaction to his work. He puzzled about the lighting and design details of the chandelier and was never quite satisfied with the end product; eventually he lost interest and moved on.

The grand organ chambers take up an entire wall of the room and organ pipes, pianos, and smaller ranks of pipes are spread throughout. The rest is a fantasy of huge proportion is made up of an assemblage of industrial salvage, wooden clocks, objects from The House on the Rock collections, artifacts from his workshops, and commissioned works. Among the several wooden clocks that Alex commissioned was a nearly five-story high "perpetual motion" clock he later called the cannonball clock. He hired woodworked/carver Harry Hichner to build the clock using cypress wood supplied by Tom Every from salvage of the wooden water tower at the Pet Milk plant in New Glarus, Wisconsin.

The Organ Room under construction, "Perpetual Motion Clock" in background

Alex continued to bring up King Ludwig II (mad King Ludwig) of Bavaria and drew inspiration from pictures of his extravagant castles and interiors. He said that Ludwig's contemporaries thought the king crazy and complained about the cost of his projects but Alex speculated that Ludwig's castles are now "The best thing they've got in that country."

There are surprises everywhere in the room and, like the rest of The House on the Rock, it is impossible to see everything in one visit. One of the things that is remarkable about this and other rooms Alex built is the density and layering of objects large and small. No matter how closely you look, there is always more; it is too much to see at one glance. Alex suffered from, or reveled in, what in art circles is termed *horror vacui*. In painting it is the obsessive desire to fill every square inch of the canvas with exquisite detail. Here in the Organ Room, and elsewhere in the attraction, Alex was continually adding objects to his displays and spent a lot of time trying to surprise and amaze visitors with sights like a steam tractor high on a shelf as if it were just a toy or a drum tree made of salvaged cheese kettles. Alex personified the description of creativity by advertising guru George Lois who said that, "The creative act is the defeat of habit by originality," and who believed that every good idea had to be outrageous.[82]

Alex came every day to oversee the work, sometimes sitting in a chair directing the operations and giving orders. The story has always circulated that even on the day he had surgery to correct a neck problem resulting from his 1972 car accident he made sure he visited the Organ Room. He woke up from surgery and as soon as he could walk he checked himself out of the hospital and drove to The House on the Rock.

Everything was overbuilt in terms of strength. There were always rumors that Alex was skirting the state building codes and proceeding surreptitiously without proper permits. When he began to build back in the 1940s things were more informal and there was no universal state building code so there was no question of getting permits. He was resistant to the idea of having to tell anybody what he was doing, but as time went on he realized that the state was not going to give him a pass and he grudgingly complied. By the 1960s he routinely obtained permits for his buildings and plans were submitted and approved by the state. In the 1970s and onward all the structures were built by professional contractors using state-approved blueprints. Since the middle 1960s he had retained engineer Rolf Killingstad who advised him and submitted plans to the state for approval. The interiors of the buildings where the displays were built were a different case, and plans could not be submitted in advance because Alex had only a general idea of where he was heading. The public was never allowed into these areas until Rolf had drawn up plans based on the final contents of the building and submitted them to the state for an occupancy permit—only then was a new area open to the public. Alex was full of bluster, bravado, and stubborn resistance when talking with his workmen about government regulations; that said, he always complied, if grudgingly, in the end.

Although the Inferno Room had been transformed into the Organ Room, he never totally abandoned his vision of making Dante's work come alive; he talked about it, drew sketches, and a few weeks before he died in 1989, still spoke about building his Inferno Room.

When the Organ Room opened to the public in late 1981, the Steampunk movement was barely on the horizon, yet this environment is an example of Steampunk. Steampunk is a branch of science fiction fascinated by steam-powered machinery and seeks to create an alternative, romantic world set in the nineteenth-century age of steam—the world of Jules Verne. Alex had no notion of the Steampunk movement, the origins of which are traced to a time after the Organ Room was created, but he worked in that spirit. The space creates a nostalgic and romantic trip through a mysterious world inhabited by objects and machines from a bygone age. There is no central focus in the room and visitors move from one set of objects, one vista to another, refocusing as they go. It is larger than one vision or one set of ideas. One of the largest works in the room and the artifact that best exemplifies the spirit of Steampunk is the Tesla, built by Tom Every. Standing next to the giant chandelier, it reaches fifty feet up to the roof.

The Tesla is a mechanical/electrical fantasy that is a transitional piece in Tom's artistic life and the place where he finished his work at The House on the Rock. The Tesla is a stand-alone creation; a fantasy assembled from his electrical and industrial savage and is the first example of Tom Every's talent for synthesizing a variety of industrial found objects into a wholly new creation. It is homage to his nineteenth- and early twentieth-century hero Nicola Tesla, a pioneer in the field of electrical engineering. Tesla had a hand in the development of alternating current and was something of a dreamer known for his dramatic electrical experiments and inventions especially the Tesla Coil. The towering assemblage evokes the spirit of Tesla and the creative ideas and experiments that earned him the popular image of the prototypical mad scientist. It is in essence a grand Steampunk creation that fits together with its own special logic—it seems to work, it seems to make sense, we have suspended disbelief about it, we want it to work; the viewer's desire to make it work in his mind welcomes him into the fantasy.

The Tesla, Great Chandelier on left

A series of accusations and a spirit of mistrust that grew between them ripped the relationship between Alex and Tom apart at the end of the work in the Organ Room. This was mostly about Tom's cavalier attitude towards money. Tom also ran afoul of the state several times regarding taxes and employee withholding. Alex became very concerned about the reputation of The House on the Rock and the possible legal consequences of what Alex referred to as "Tom's skullduggery." The two egos clashed one more time; in the end there were lawsuits back and forth ending in Tom's conviction for contractor fraud, which landed him in jail. These events were a source of bitterness and anger for Tom that he carried with him for years. He blamed Alex for all of his self-defeating behaviors. Nothing can take away his achievements at The House on the Rock or all that he learned while being given the freedom to create with Alex Jordan. Every went on to reinvent himself under the moniker of Dr. Evermor, becoming a well-known visionary sculptor; in later years he softened his feelings toward The House on the Rock and Alex Jordan.[83]

In the Organ Room, Alex created an overwhelming fantasy environment on an industrial scale; the room exceeded his expectations, and he was pleased with this accomplishment. Although he would sit for hours in front of the great Carousel, he still considered the Organ Room his best work; it touched something deep inside him and exposed the source of his imagination and its curious turns. In this room his originality and vision were at their best; there is no prototype, he was not imitating anything—he wasn't making a carousel only bigger and better, or a Streets of Yesterday—this was completely new.

The source of this dark, mysterious, sensual aesthetic is deeper in his life history than he could admit—coming from the rich, romantic and sensual life of his childhood influences and imagination. He had done everything he could to escape from his strict Catholic upbringing. He was rebellious by nature and bridled under the domination of the strict Catholic household of his mother and the regulations of his education. When his mother passed away in 1969 he immediately removed some of the last vestiges of religious practice from the property and announced, "That is the end of religion at The House on the Rock." It may well have been the end in his mind—but not so fast. His Catholic background had a profound effect on his imagination, and as sociologist Andrew Greeley points out, "Catholics live in an enchanted world, a world of statues and holy water, stained glass, and votive candles, saints, and religious medals, rosary beads and holy pictures."[84] Greeley believes that Catholic culture shapes the imagination of those who grow up in this milieu and has a lasting effect on creative people even if they later reject and are hostile to religion. He calls it "an enchanted imagination." Alex did reject the insular Catholic world he grew up in but could not escape the effects it had on his imagination; his fascination with Dante's *Divine Comedy* and other religious elements was not accidental. His earliest influences, promoted by his mother, were of this enchanted and sensual world of Catholicism that he was taught to value and which became his childish worldview—these were the seeds of his adult imagination. The thread of this belief system continued to wind through his creations in the Organ Room. He could escape the Catholic world physically and even intellectually but it remained deeply a part of who he was. A religious Catholic he was not, but the aesthetics of the Church were woven into his fabric. In the Organ Room he built what amounts to a secular church—a church with pseudo-religious trappings, a shrine to the fantasy of an age long ago with statues and organ music and a grand space to boot—godless though it may be, still a church.

CHAPTER 10

MR. JORDAN'S CABINET OF CURIOSITIES

Alex Jordan filled mysterious rooms with a mixture of objects that defy description and at times read like a senseless juxtaposition of unrelated things: there seems to be no logical order, always the unexpected or the strange mixed in—and most of it unlabeled. It all works to create a sense of confusion in those looking for a common theme, as if The House on the Rock were a theme park. Those who open up without question and drink it in are rewarded with a sense of child-like wonder. It's easier to say what The House on the Rock *is not*, rather than what it is. But still, the fair questions remain: What is this? How does it fit into society? Is this quintessentially American?

There is in human nature a desire to collect and for some, the gathering and display of the rare and unusual objects is an all-consuming passion. This deeply human activity is a universal archetype held in the dark recesses of our souls and shared in common among peoples and across time. During the last 400 years European collectors have followed a pathway starting with

Cabinet of Curiosities, *tromp-l'oeil* painting by Domenico Remps, late 1600s.

Cabinets of Curiosities and developing into the modern day idea of a museum. American culture further developed the European traditions of collecting.

The first Cabinets of Curiosities in Europe, forerunners of the modern museum, date from the 1600s. The image "Cabinet of Curiosities, tromp-l'oeil painting by Domenico Remps, late 1600s" shows an artist's rendition of a 1667 cabinet.[85]

In the seventeenth century natural science was in its infancy, and in the beginning the Cabinets of Curiosities were made up primarily of wonders or oddities from the natural world. Gradually collectors began to add not only objects from the natural world, but also art works and then anything that struck them as bizarre or wonderful. The Cabinets reflected the personality of the collector, and it wasn't long before the cabinets became entire rooms filled with wonders. In Germany these rooms were called *Wunderkammer,* meaning chambers of marvels. Although these collections were no longer cabinets as we think of them but actual rooms they continued to be referred to as Cabinets of Curiosities.

The Cabinet of Francesco Calzolari, 1662

These rooms, filled with natural wonders and oddities, were very much private, usually collected by the aristocracy, and only seen by their inner circle. Some collections became large and varied as collectors began to accumulate on a full-time basis and built buildings to house their artifacts; they even divided their collections into a series of themed rooms. The collectors began to exhibit their curiosities in such a way as to lead the viewer from "one object to the next, each more bizarre and wonderful than the last. For wonder was the keynote of the Cabinets of Curiosities."[86]

Athanasius Kircher Collection, late 1600s
(Courtesy of Department of Special Collections and University Archives,
Stanford University Libraries)

A view of the work the grandest collector of the seventeenth century, Athanasius Kircher (in the illustration on the previous page), shows how big these collections became, fillings whole rooms with objects of wonder. Kircher was not satisfied displaying objects of wonder, he enhanced his collections by including his own inventions and special effects like his talking statue which he operated himself, speaking through a long tube from a hidden room, amazing visitors with a voice from who knew where.

Kircher's Voice Tube, middle 1600s
(Courtesy of Department of Special Collections and University Archives,
Stanford University Libraries)

Kircher was one of the most brilliant minds of his age, and what he added to his Cabinet of Curiosities was not only the odd or unexpected but also entertainment. He invented a hydraulic organ complete with animations for the entertainment of his guests. Kircher was not satisfied only to induce a sense of wonder from the variety of his exotic collections but took the idea a step further introducing an element of entertainment.

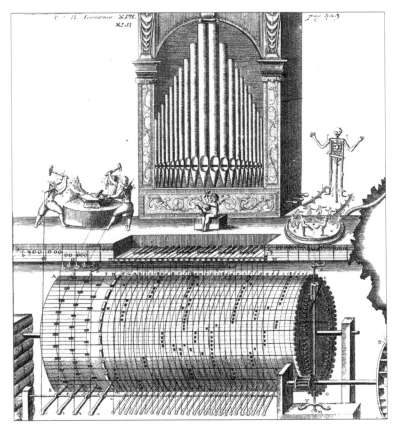

Kircher's Hydraulic Organ, middle 1600s
(Courtesy of Department of Special Collections and University Archives,
Stanford University Libraries)

In the 1700s and into the 1800s, science began to make important discoveries, and the idea of Cabinets of Curiosities divided into two separate identities. The natural history museum as we know it developed from these cabinets. The Cabinets of Curiosities themselves continued on, still exhibiting the odd, the mysterious, and the intriguing. As science became important the cabinets were "reduced to the level of imperfect science" and were considered vulgar and common, popular entertainment. The museum is where scientific truth came to reside. With the Enlightenment of the eighteenth century and the development of the scientific method the Cabinets of Curiosities were further relegated to the position of unsophisticated entertainment.

Charles Wilson Peale and his Museum, 1786

In America Charles Wilson Peale founded the first true museum of any consequence, Peale's American Museum, in 1786. It was a collection of natural wonders as well as fine art. Peale made a serious attempt to document his collections and present scientific data about his artifacts. Peale's museum failed financially and many of the contents of the museum were sold to P. T. Barnum who put together an attraction part museum and part sideshow and something like a Cabinet of Curiosities.

In the 1860s one of the most popular attractions in Manhattan was Barnum's American Museum. In the then short history of American museums, Barnum's museum was an original. It claimed to offer 850,000 "interesting curiosities" as described in Barnum's pamphlet "An Illustrated Catalogue and Guide Book" which Barnum sold for ten cents at the entrance of his museum. The cover reads, "Being an illustrated review of the principal objects of interest in the extensive establishment, and useful to the visitor for purposes of reference, entertainment and instruction." The ads for the sale of this booklet declare, "Every visitor should own one."[87]

There are curious parallels between Barnum's museum and The House on the Rock. Alex did not consciously follow Barnum or his American Museum Guidebook; there is not a copy of the Guidebook among his papers or books. In fact there are no books or articles about Barnum anywhere in the archives. But they were certainly working along the same lines, and they are both truly American in their approach. For all his use of modern techniques and materials, Alex Jordan had one foot in the nineteenth century; his ideas for exhibiting his collections were not based on the European model but were really more like Barnum. Jordan is a good deal less brash in his exhibitions than Barnum, and there are certainly no dwarfs, deformed people, bearded ladies, Siamese twins, or mermaid skeletons on display at The House on the Rock.

To illustrate the parallels between the two attractions, here is a general description of Barnum's museum from the Kunhardt 1995 biography, *P. T. Barnum: America's Greatest Showman*: "Instead of devoting whole floors to minerals or shells or stuffed birds, as in other museums, Barnum sprinkled in unrelated and fascinating objects wherever possible: Medieval armor, funny mirrors, an autograph collection, a piece of trans-Atlantic cable, a collection of shoes, the arm of a pirate, a powerful magnet, and also presented historical artifacts such as the complete state carriage of the late Dowager Queen of England."

This was not a true museum as we think of them—this was entertainment. It was "the juxtaposition of the unexpected that made his museum so delectably entertaining, capable of being enjoyed by everyone from a foreign-speaking, working-class immigrant to the most educated member of New York's elite."[88] Barnum's museum came under fire in *The Nation* magazine for being a "mixed up and confusing heap" of curiosities, a criticism occasionally leveled at Alex Jordan's House on the Rock, "the valuable and the worthless mixed together" and the collections chaotic.[89] Barnum fired back that his museum was not government funded and he needed to support his family—he needed to make it popular and interesting. The fact is that both Barnum and Jordan were combining and juxtaposing their exhibits for one purpose—to "banish boredom." What they both had in common was that they wanted to increase attendance and make more money so they could get even more new and exotic collections. Barnum was an impresario, an extroverted entertainer, a showman, and shameless self-promoter. Although Alex was always a fan of the excessive, he was an inward-turning person who preferred to hide in the shadows; not a confidence man, he was always square in his business dealings. He was often hyperbolic and if he exaggerated a bit—that was entertainment. Barnum made money from his deceptions and even from the exposure of his falsehoods while Alex Jordan felt embarrassed and mortified his.

Until the Barnum Museum, art and collectables were the province of the European aristocracy and were not available to the common man. What is typically American about this new approach is that the collections were available for everyone, not just the wealthy or highborn. Anybody with twenty-five cents could see the wonders of the Barnum American Museum. In reality Barnum had created more of an attraction than a museum and sensible people recognized the difference, and so it is with The House on the Rock. Alex often declared, "This is not a museum," and whenever a craftsmen in his employ became too fussy about what he thought of as unnecessary detail he was quick to caution, "This is not the Smithsonian!" It was all about entertainment. Alex Jordan built at The House on the Rock an attraction that is quintessentially American and the true descendant of the Cabinets of Curiosities.

Alex hated to be compared to or mentioned in the same breath as P.T. Barnum who is usually associated with fakery, exaggerated promotions and tasteless human spectacles. He called any comparison to Barnum, "an insult." He never spoke of Barnum except in pejorative terms. He certainly wanted no part of what is the popular image of Barnum summed up in the statement, "There's a sucker born every minute," or in the sideshow image of his later years.[90] That said—both were showmen who were dedicated to entertainment.

Barnum and Jordan worked under the spell of the same archetype, an archetype reaching back to Europe but boldly American; they were responding to a primal and universal need to collect and display objects of wonder.

The House on the Rock is one of two important and puzzling large-scale Cabinets of Curiosities in the United States. The other well-known example is The Museum of Jurassic Technology in Los Angeles that was founded by David and Diana Wilson in 1988. The Museum of Jurassic Technology is a Cabinet of Curiosities containing collections and exhibits, some of which are made up of authentic artifacts while others are products of imagination—things that could have been or should have been. A stink ant, a bat frozen in a sold lead wall, human horns, a scale model of Noah's ark, microscopic fruit stone carvings. It is a place of amazement and wonder but disconcerting—there is a sense that something is just not right. It is a place where the real and the imagined coexist side by side in an ambiguous setting that has all the credible markings of a museum, but viewers are never sure whether what is exhibited is real or imagined and in the end may come to the conclusion that it makes no difference. The question of authentic, real, or imagined seems here to be beside the point—irony and reality are intertwined.[91]

The House on the Rock and the Museum of Jurassic Technology have little in common aside from being modern-day examples of Cabinets of Curiosities— they come from different points of view. Although in both cases the authentic and the imagined are side by side in a museum-like setting, The House on the Rock offers few labels and fewer explanations while The Museum of Jurassic Technology relies on the descriptive narrative of information boards. There is no complex intellectual or ironic intent in the work of Alex Jordan. It is pure collecting for amazement—make of it what you will, they are two very different Cabinets and two very different intentions.

The House on the Rock is the true descendent of The Cabinets of Curiosities in the American tradition, and to use Barnum's words "a haunt of all things wonderful," mysterious, unexpected, jarring, challenging.

CHAPTER 11

MR. JORDAN'S IMAGINARIUM

Any attempt to gain perspective on Alex Jordan's collecting habits is difficult. This private man did not talk much about his collecting and even less about his childhood or his motivations. His background has features in common with other grandiose and obsessive collectors: the forceful and domineering father he never seemed able to please and his mother's early doting of him aside (she was reputed to be emotionally remote). We can only speculate about the exact relationship between Alex and his parents and its effect on his mature years.

Behaviorists find that obsessive collecting is sometimes a symptom of a need to make up for a lack of nurturing in childhood. The collector finds objects more reliable than people, even as the neglected and shy child finds refuge in toys and imaginative worlds. There was always something of a child in Alex, not in the Peter Pan sense but as the lonely boy with the toys he relied on, and the tricks and escapes he used to gain approval. Psychiatrist Werner Muensterberger in his scholarly study, *Collecting: An Unruly Passion*, points out: "Like the dedicated collector, the child, absorbed with his toys, 'dreams his way not only into a remote and bygone world, but at the same time into a better one.'"[92] The bygone world of The Streets of Yesterday, the early industrial mechanical fantasy that is the Organ Room and the improbable and visionary Carousel are the huge toy box of his collectibles. "What else are collectibles but toys grown-ups take seriously?"[93] Muensterberger further points out, "We recognize one trait shared by all true collectors—that there is simply no saturation point."[94] But Alex did not collect for the love of the object, nor did he obsess about getting all the varieties of a category of collectibles; he felt no need to fill in the missing gaps in his collections but valued his acquisitions not for the objects themselves as much as for their possibilities as objects for exhibition. He had no difficulty exhibiting rare antiques and found or fabricated artifacts together because his collecting was not intellectual, not museum-like—it was wondrous and romantic. He did not hoard his objects like a jealous mogul; all that he amassed was for the show and it was all for approval. And when the public or the media approved, shy and reserved, he took his quite pleasure in the background. These deeper and darker paths of inquiry into his motivations beyond showmanship and the complex and intriguing issues of his tendencies and their origins have passed away with him, but the evidence of his struggles is clearly in his work. His fondest hope was: admire the collection—admire the collector, but at a distance.[95]

Alex continued to check off in his notebooks things that he always wanted to build, and while he was dividing his attention between his other big projects—the Carousel and the Organ Room—he also began to work on the building he originally thought would be for the grand organ. The stepped roofs of the building stretched down the hillside enclosing the empty theater-like space. This room became a canvas where he made real the ideas he had been toying with for a long time.

First, Alex pursued what must be considered, judging from the great number of drawings in his notebooks and his talking about it, something from his "bucket list." He would eventually call it "The Colossus of Ivan the Terrible," and although it is a prop, he still was fond of calling it the "World's Largest Cannon."

For years Alex had sketched a variety of cannon designs in his notebooks and did a great deal of research on the subject. Sid Boyum suggested the cannon be patterned after the one in the movie, *The Pride and the Passion*; some details on the muzzle come from this source—Sid would later claim the design as his own. The design was, in fact, collaboration between Alex and the author. Alex was fascinated with the process and had his assistant manager, Neil Hanson, take photos of the progress on a nearly daily basis. It was at this time that the falling out with Sid Boyum became pronounced.

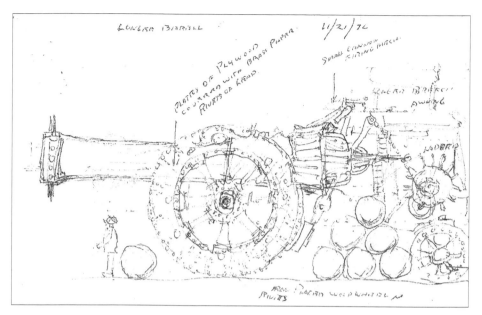

Alex Jordan drawing of the Cannon

Alex would occasionally bring Sid along on his daily trips to The House on the Rock; he was a sight to see in his overcoat, slightly hunched over, chewing on a fast disappearing cigar, a curmudgeonly character, creative, full of stories (some true), an excessive lover of cats (more than thirty at the end), best met upwind but always leaving behind him a buzz of remarks and laughter. Coming through the unfinished buildings with Alex one day in 1978 at the time when the steam tractors had just been moved into the unfinished Carousel building—the cannon was half done, the Organ Room still a cavernous space where Tom Every was working—he growled, "This is not The House on the Rock anymore, I don't know what he's [Alex] doing here!" If there was a discernible turning point at which the decline in their relationship was evident, it might have been then. Sid, and others, might have wanted The House on the Rock to be the old way—a small roadside attraction, mostly the House, but that was over, and Alex had very much bigger things in mind.[96]

The finished Cannon

Alex for his part was very pleased with the Cannon, named the building the Cannon Room, and had a viewing window built where guests could see his creation in the unfinished room. He told me on the last day of construction: "Always in my life there never was enough, whether it was cigarettes, or booze, or anything, whatever else—nothing was ever enough. Finally, something that is enough."

In keeping with his general plan to offer something for all tastes, Alex commissioned woodworker/carver Harry Hitchner to build a lofty doll castle as a counterpoint to the cannon and installed it opposite "The Colossus." Harry fabricated it in his workshop and delivered it to a craftsperson in Madison where the finishing touches of velvet and thousands of faux pearls were added. Alex tinkered with the castle for years, adding pieces and extra lighting until it nearly fell over from its own weight. Hitchner had been working under contract for Alex; he started out by building a smaller wall-mounted wooden clock that was installed in the Organ Room. He was also involved in a large project in the Organ

Room that did not go well at the end and is typical of the woes of a number of independent craftspeople that Alex commissioned. The project (CHAPTER 9) was the enormous (five story) perpetual motion clock. In reality it was run by a small electric motor. The apparent source power was to be a number of wooden balls that were lifted to the ceiling by the clock's motion and provided power on their way down. Harry, an aeronautical engineer by training, designed the components of the gigantic clock and fabricated them in his shop. After fabrication he delivered the components to the site and assembled them. There was no written agreement between Alex and Harry, which was not unusual. The huge clock was gradually assembled in the Organ Building and Harry began to realize that he was past the money—he had put a great deal of work and money into the project. To finish, there was more to be built, including the wooden balls, but Alex was not going to listen. Harry could not afford to continue. He also felt that he was being underpaid, and did not want to do any more projects for Alex at the old price. This led to the day when Harry was escorted to his vehicle and asked to leave, even as the huge clock remained so close to completion.[97]

Alex thought he could finish the clock and got some basketballs to use in place of the wooden balls. Disaster followed as the angry Alex insisted that his tinkering with the clock and the basketballs would work, despite repeated, and sometimes humorous failures— he really needed Harry there to finish the project. The basketballs were not going to work no matter how much Alex gave commands and there were also further adjustments that needed to be made. Finally, after much steaming and cursing he gave up; the clock stands silent today, a monument to Alex's stubbornness and temper. After Alex passed away, an employee climbed the face of the clock and set the time to 4:15—the reported time of his death.[98]

The perpetual motion clock debacle is typical of the experience that a good number of contract craftspeople had with Alex. There were some notable exceptions, people who seemed to have no trouble with him, but more often the end would be some variation of Harry Hitchner's experience. Alex had an inborn suspicion of contractors and was always on the lookout for those who might try to cheat him. His father had warned him to be tough so people wouldn't run all over him. Part of the problem came from the fact that there was nothing written down and Alex's expectations and vision were not always in line with the image the craftsperson had in mind. And then it was Alex, so he was pushing and squeezing all he could out of the project, making additions and changes that individually were small but incrementally added up to sizeable construction expense that he expected the craftsperson to absorb. And he would not listen to complaining or adjust the price he was willing to pay. To be sure, he had some experiences in which his suspicion and caution were well placed—the Perpetual Motion Clock was not one of them.

With the Doll Castle and the Cannon in place, the room was still called The Cannon Room but that too would change before the room opened in 1982. Alex was puzzling for a way to display his collection of over 650 antique bisque dolls when Tom Every came up with a series of curved "I" beams he had salvaged and suggested that they would make good curved ramps for the Cannon Room. Alex got the idea of wrapping the ramps around two multi-storied carousels and so the doll carousels became the centerpiece of the room now called The Doll Carousels. He furnished the multi-level carousels with scaled-down horses and custom-made creatures from his imagination in a smaller version of the grand Carousel next door; on these he placed his doll collection. He then had built a series of centaurs and female nudes to crown the upper carousel to give it a little "punch."

Doll Carousel

As a final exclamation point in the room, and to "throw a curve at them" he had the author create "The Four Horsemen of the Apocalypse" in monumental proportion. One of the books on the shelf in the sculpture part of the workshop was a volume containing prints of the woodcuts of the sixteenth-century German artist Albrecht Durer. Alex took great pleasure in examining the prints and was especially taken with Durer's "Four Horsemen;" he always said that one day we would make one better than Durer, whatever that meant. He was ebullient at the start of the project and said that this work would one day make the author famous and rich. He was excited about the work and tickled about some of the stories that came along with it, among them that the local undertaker, who also pumped LP gas part time, came into the workshop when the piece was nearly done and confirmed that the carotid arteries hanging down from the severed heads slung over the saddle of the Disease figure were indeed anatomically correct. Alex greatly appreciated this sculpture and uncharacteristically had a bronze plaque engraved crediting the author.[99]

Everything Alex couldn't get into the Organ Room he fitted into The Doll Carousels; the room turned into a giant fantasy toy box filled with random items from Alex's list including a giant concrete rendition of "Old Man Willow" inspired by J. R.R. Tolkcin's *The Fellowship of the Ring*. All of the artifacts in the room are unique creations; there is no synthesis of ready-made objects into fantasy pieces as in the Organ Room and there is no understandable theme as in The Streets of Yesterday or the grand Carousel. Although the Doll Carousels themselves seem to set the theme for the room, the disparate objects in the space create an atmosphere of incongruity. This room, like the rest of the attraction, is The Imaginarium of Alex Jordan—a place devoted to the recesses of his imagination, where he brought to life images and fantasies with no particular order or logic. The room is less like an exhibition space and more like a view into the random thoughts and images of a creative mind.

The Four Horsemen of the Apocalypse

The dollhouse collection, like so many others, started with the purchase of one and then another custom-made house that Alex happened upon. These original few houses were put on display and drew favorable comments from visitors. Several employees pointed out to him that it would be cheaper to have dollhouses built in the shop and that all of the miniature furniture and architectural details were easily available. If he was going to have a collection of dollhouses, he needed to have the largest and best collection in the world. He did what he always did first: researched dollhouses, scoured the shelves of used bookstores for books, read all he could find, and talked to collectors and hobbyists—his research convinced him that somewhere in the vicinity of 250 dollhouses would make his collection the largest by far.

The Carousel project was in its final stages and the shop was emptied of the hundreds of carousel animals that were installed on the grand carousel. Alex hired Virginia Reynolds, first to assist in the painting of the final carousel animals for the grand Carousel and then the figures for the Doll Carousels.

He now asked her to undertake the dollhouse project. She soon had her own growing corner of the workshop, assisted by several helpers, including her daughter Cherie Reynolds Greek. Senior painter Jim McKahan was pleased to have Virginia and crew in the shop. Alex occasionally mentioned the dollhouse project he was thinking about and said that Jim would have plenty of work painting the houses. Jim was not in the least interested in painting dollhouses and was pleased when Virginia showed a real passion for the project—it got him off the hook. His worry was a moot point because Jim was finished with his work at The House on the Rock and would soon wander off.

As with so many of Alex's large projects, the planning and production of the dollhouse collection was a collaboration. The original idea, the vision, was Alex's but the building, detailing and management of this huge project was left mostly in Virginia's hands. He came in each day, as was his habit, and looked at the work, sometimes taking the time to stop and visit (especially if there happened to be an open bag of junk food nearby) and track the progress. The dollhouse production area became one of his regular stops on his pass through. The style of the designs spanned from early American architecture through the beginning of the twentieth century in keeping with the nostalgic ambience of The House on the Rock.

Some houses were constructed from pre-made kits and then were customized, but most of the houses in the collection were built from scratch. In the heyday of construction, Alex hired an independent woodworkers shop to produce the shells of custom-designed houses, which were then finished in The House on the Rock workshop. It once again became difficult to walk through the shop without turning sideways as the number of houses grew and then were stacked, in some cases up to the ceiling. Each house was given appropriate architectural detailing, painting, papering, and electrification and then fitted with period furnishings. The care is so fine that it even includes mice in the attic. As usual, Alex oversaw the project, sometimes with detailed instructions and other times merely general directions. And in a typical Jordan move, he had a miniature brothel built for the collection— certainly the only dollhouse brothel anywhere—still the bad boy, still trying to shock.

Dollhouses

In 1985 after some mottling around about design, the world's largest collection of dollhouses (265) was installed in a dark labyrinthine series of corridors displayed in low light and the glow from their own internal fixtures.

What to make of all this? The dollhouses are yet another venture following the familiar pattern of vision, massive factory-like production, and then the display of a collection of exhausting proportions. It is not wise to make too little or too much of the deeper meaning, but the extremes always are food for thought. It is not enough to say that he made these collections and displays so he could earn money from visitors in order to make more displays. He was, after all, feeding on the approval of the public, there is something deeper here, something childlike, some emptiness he wanted to fill. Jane Smiley, *New York Times* contributor and Pulitzer Prize winner put it this way:

> In fact, astonishment seems to be the main goal of all the displays and all the literature at The House on the Rock. In the place darkness prevails. The rooms containing collections have no light of their own—only the pieces themselves are lighted, often from within…The sheer abundance of objects

is impressive, and the warmth most of the objects exude, the way that the toys ask to be played with, for example, makes the displays inherently inviting. But almost from the beginning it is too much…everything is simply massed together, and Alex Jordan comes to seem like the manifestation of pure American acquisitiveness, and acquisitiveness of a strangely boyish kind as if he had finalized all his desires in childhood and never grown into any others.[100]

Alex was not prepared for the increase in visitors in the early 1980s that resulted from the opening of the Carousel and Organ Room and the publicity these new exhibits generated. Reporters from newspapers and magazines as well as television hounded the attraction. Increased attendance meant more revenue—but also brought with it new problems. In the days before the Carousel and other additions, visitors stayed an hour or maybe an hour and a half and then they were on their way; now it was two hours and more. By the later half of the 1980s attendance increased dramatically; it was not unusual for guests to stay for more than three hours.

The strain on the infrastructure of The House on the Rock worried Alex, and he tried to lower attendance by increasing the price of admission, but this strategy failed to reduce the number of guests—in fact, attendance grew. It was so crowded that it was difficult to move through the tour and employees in some of the areas found they could not take breaks at the scheduled time because it would take too long to elbow their way through the throng. There were long waits to buy tickets and not enough restrooms and guests wanted to get something to eat.

Alex turned his attention to these problems and built new restrooms, a ticketing area, and eventually two small indoor/outdoor restaurants. In the early years he had allowed the installation of a number of soda machines near the entrance area, and he became the largest retailer of pop in southwestern Wisconsin. He became irritated with the pop bottles and the labor he had to expend on clean up, so one day he threw them all out. Alex never liked the idea of gift shops, thinking that this would cheapen the attraction, but in keeping with the trend of the times and with the encouragement of Steve and Elizabeth Murray he gave in and allowed a small gift shop. Elizabeth was now (middle 1980s) his business assistant, keeping the books for him while Steve managed one of the restaurants as well as the growing retail areas. The gift shop expanded and Alex added an area that he called The Artists' Village where retail space was rented to craftspeople, a reminder of the days twenty years before when he invited artists to exhibit their work at The House on the Rock. He made sure that there were alternative pathways by which guests were able to bypass the retail areas; he grew used to all this and in later years enjoyed sitting in the shade at an outdoor table eating a bowl of ice cream. But he was never really at peace about the overtly commercial appearance, and he told me so saying, "I'd rather give them all a doughnut and a cup of coffee and send them on their way."

These new outdoor areas gave him a space that he now had workers fill to overflowing with greenery and flowering plants. There had always been flowers at The House on the Rock; Alex allowed the cleaning staff to buy a few plants in the spring for pots on the sundeck of the House. He himself had no patience with plants; one season he bought some plastic tulips and stuck them in the ground in the old abandoned Duck Pond walkway where they could be seen from the House ramp. They stayed there through August, dusty and drooping until someone pulled them up and threw them away.

In 1983 Alex hired Ron Boley as his head gardener and as usual when Jordan turned to something, he went overboard. In the next few years he built a complex of greenhouses and support buildings to produce and care for a superabundance of flowers and greenery. Alex and Ron banged their heads together over methods and ideas. Early on Ron had gotten an indication of how things might go when he climbed up on the roof of the Mill House and started to clean up the mess of dead vegetation from old plantings and droppings left there by the now departed goat Lucifer. He had his head down, working, not expecting to see Alex up there on the roof. He heard something and turned around just as Jordan let out a string of curses, shouting that Ron was trying to turn the place into, "A f#####g golf course."[101]

And they moved on from there.

Somehow they found a way to work together, and Ron stayed with The House on the Rock the rest of Alex's life and beyond for a total of thirty years, creating in the process the largest container garden in the state. The problem with Alex always was that when he got an idea into his head, in Ron's words, "He just went ape." And so it was with the gardens as he began a building program at the workshops adding yet more greenhouses and temperature-controlled buildings to store exotic plants in the cold season. He also built a climate controlled building just for the care of his favorite flower, the amaryllis—8,000 of them. It is difficult to say whether Alex really had a truly favorite flower. Ron later said that he though that the amaryllis was the only flower Alex could identify. Whatever Alex's preferences were, through temperature control and careful management, Ron was able to have amaryllis in bloom for the long period of the tourist season. The greenhouses produced thousands of plants and flowers through the season providing a colorful display of which Alex, his black thumb and all, was justifiably proud.

The Container Garden

Alex turned his attention to the design of pots large and small for the increasing number of flowering plants Ron was producing. At the end of 1983, the author produced a full-scale prototype of the large pots (*sans* dragons) that now line The House on the Rock driveway. The design of many of the pots originated with a strawberry pot that Alex's mother had that was at The House on the Rock in the 1960s. He brought this pot into the shop at the beginning of the process and said he wanted a "really big one." He got the idea for adding the lizards and dragons from ancient Chinese pottery Alex had seen in one of the many books lying around the shop. After consultation with Ron Boley, Alex contracted them out their manufacture. The huge pots are typical Jordan pieces—massive and exotic with their lizards and dragons writhing over the contours. They proved very popular with visitors and Alex installed them, in various sizes and configurations, at the highway entrance and along the driveway into the attraction as well as in the parking lots.

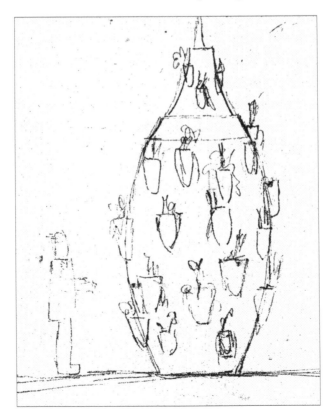

Alex Jordan drawing of large pot

Chapter 12

"Ah-h-h"

The idea of The Infinity Room originated in Alex's mind sometime in the 1940s. In a 1962 interview he referred to The Infinity Room as the "nose cone." The first drawings are of a square-looking structure ending with a huge fireplace a short distance out balanced over Observation Rock, a stone pillar twenty feet out from the House. Later designs show a cantilevered building constructed of timbers and glass extending out from the living room. This design also called for a huge fireplace. He reflected on it at the time: "The Infinity Room, ah-h-h, that's a great one. That's the most beautiful idea I've had. I really want to do it. It's given to very few to do a thing like that. First you have to have the location. I'd start here on Deershelter…and run on out sixty feet cantilevered out over the valley…"

Alex continued to make drawings of The Infinity Room and as the idea grew, he began to realize the limitations of wood construction as the dimensions of the building increased. The Infinity Room remained a project on the back burner for more than thirty years; Alex periodically talked about building it and hired several artists to make conceptual drawings of his ideas, sketches he eventually used along with his own designs when the time came to go ahead with the project. In 1962, he talked about his plans: "It will be my biggest fireplace. And the room will have what amounts to a picture window as long as two bowling alleys end to end. Right now, from the island [Observation Rock] you can throw a stone that will land at the bottom of the valley. From The Infinity Room you will just about be able to hit the valley floor by dropping a stone straight down—you'll be that far out in space."[102]

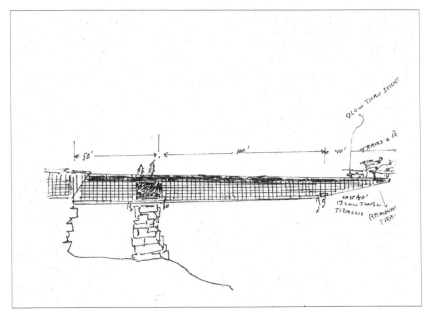

Alex Jordan drawing of The Infinity Room

The Infinity Room is another example of Alex's desire to stretch everything and everyone to the extreme. But wooden-beam construction could be cantilevered only so far. The House and all of the buildings until the early 1970s were wood-frame construction but as Alex's ideas became grander and his need for broader spaces increased, he turned to custom designed metal buildings and the use of structural steel. When Tom Every arrived on the scene with his aggressive methods of steel fabrication and "power on" attitude, he introduced Alex to a new range of possibilities. The serious challenges involved in the completion of the Carousel and the Organ Room demonstrated to Alex an expanded way of thinking about construction. After Tom's demise his sub-contractor, Dave Nelson, took over the challenge of construction and custom iron fabrication for Alex. Dave's crew of ironworkers were responsible for the erection of buildings and the fabrication of structural interior features for the rest of Alex's career. One day in August of 1984 Alex asked Dave Nelson to stop by The House on the Rock office; he showed Dave some of the artist's drawings for The Infinity Room structure and asked him if he could build it. Dave assured Alex that with his crew of fearless ironworkers and the proper engineering it could be done. The structure is the result of a bond of trust among three energetic and skilled forces: Alex Jordan, Dave Nelson and crew, and engineer Rolf Killingstad. Rolf had advised and consulted on engineering issues for The House on the Rock for twenty years by the time The Infinity Room project came along; during that time he also developed a relationship of trust with Dave Nelson and his workers.

Alex visited Rolf and showed him the artists' conceptual drawings of the project. Rolf was amazed at the daring scope of the idea; he initially expressed his doubts and spent some time trying to talk Alex out of it, but Alex insisted he should conquer the technical problems and forge ahead. The first set of drawings that Rolf submitted to Alex were for a building that was 160 feet long; Alex was very disappointed and said that wasn't long enough—it had to be at least 200 feet long. Rolf returned to his drawing board and gave Alex what he wanted. The building is over 200 feet in length, the last 140 feet of which is cantilevered above Wyoming Valley, stretching the properties of steel and engineering skill to the limit.[103]

The Infinity Room under construction

The construction method was as unique as the building itself. First, a concrete and steel bridge was built from Deershelter Rock, upon which the House is built, out twenty feet to Observation Rock; beyond this point The Infinity Room balances unsupported. The ironworkers employed a brace-box method of construction, a telescoping system in which each section was built inside the previous section, slid out, and welded in place. All of this work was done hanging in mid-air with a safety net suspended below. The structure was built to withstand the stresses of wind and weather as well as the weight of visitors accommodating 200 pounds per square foot. As a test, a 2000-pound weight was suspended from the end of the completed structure, which resulted in only three-eighths-inch deflection. Don Martin installed over 3,000 windowpanes on the cantilevered sides and constructed a glass-topped table at the far end of the room through which visitors can peer to the forest floor below. During construction Alex visited every day and walked out, shuffling along on the skeletal steel structure, oblivious as usual to the height, monitoring progress and talking to the workmen. Construction took only fourteen months to complete and the room opened in October 1985. It far exceeded Alex's dreams.

The Infinity Room

This was the last great architectural project for Alex; most of his work since building the Mill House in 1968 involved interior environments such as The Streets of Yesterday, grand theatrical showmanship like the Carousel, and culminated in the fantasy ambience of the Organ Room. Now with The Infinity Room he returned to architecture one last time, making a dramatic statement and completing his dream for the House and again opening up a panoramic, and dizzying, view of the countryside below and beyond. Thirty years before Alex added his own verse to Don Blanding's book-length poem *Vagabond's House*:

> One long thin room will hang in space
> And at the end there'll be a place,
> For a kindly saint as a figurehead
> To turn away the thin heights dread,
> And to keep all fearful things away.

The fearful things? The only fearful things for the seventy-one-year-old Alex Jordan in 1985 were the sands of time.

CHAPTER 13

"Do not go gentle into that good night, Old age should burn and rave at the close of day...."[104]

As 1986 began, Alex suffered increasingly from health problems related to his life-long heart condition. It became more difficult for him to find the energy to manage projects that were underway or that he was planning—but he soldiered on. He developed a new approach to astonishing his guests; this new idea is exemplified in three of his final projects, two of which were left unfinished at the time of his death: The Circus Room, The Whale Building (now called The Heritage of the Sea), and the Transportation Building (now called The Tribute to Nostalgia). Only the Circus Room was essentially complete at the time of his death in November of 1989, although the Circus Orchestra itself was not operational until the spring of 1990.

He now decided that an unbelievably huge central prop would dominate his major rooms, with smaller displays along the outer walls of the building. His tendency toward gigantism was evident in the grand Carousel and in the Organ Room where a massive environment tends to overwhelm the viewer. The effect that this had on the public was not lost on Alex. He moved on to scale up giant size the pots and vases he scattered around the driveway and garden spaces. The huge cannon in the Doll Carousels fits the bill as a giant prop, but it is by no means central to the room. In his late projects, 1986–89, he indulged his appetite for gigantic props that exhibit not only fantastic scenes but also demonstrate his power and resources. He had collected massive numbers of artifacts to wow the public and would continue to do so right to the end, but Alex was conscious of his need to continually top himself, and gigantism was the way forward.

164

The Circus is dominated by a circus wagon of epic proportions. A giant whale-like creature 175-feet long in a death struggle with a giant squid overwhelms The Whale Building. Plans for the Transportation Building show a five-story steam tractor filling the airplane hanger-size room. Alex was no longer satisfied to present dazzling artifacts such as the grand Carousel as a centerpiece. He now stretched his visionary artifacts beyond the limits of credibility and entered into the realm of pure fantasy. There is no real whale of the size, much less with the amalgamated features, of the whale then under construction at The House on the Rock. The Circus Wagon would be nearly impossible to move, aside from the fact that it would collapse under its own weight. The planned five-story steam tractor exceeds the limits of reality, practical engineering, and usefulness.

Alex always had an interest in the allure and the romance of the circus and took some inspiration from the Florida trip he took with Tom and Eleanor Every in the middle 1970s. He was fascinated by the Ringling Circus Museum and walked through the exhibits that included circus costumes, posters, wagons and miniature circus artifacts (CHAPTER 9). It may have been there in the circus collections of the Ringling Museum that the seeds of the idea for the Circus Room at The House on the Rock began to take shape. Years later he would suggest building concrete banyan trees like those found on the grounds of the museum.

In the 1980s when a number of miniature circuses became available, Alex jumped at the opportunity to add these to his collections. The miniature circuses consisted of hundreds of thousands of pieces ranging in scale from one-eighth inch to one foot, to one inch to one foot; the big top tent in the one-inch scale is over thirty-feet long. They came from Ann and Lou Kretschmer and included was a model, accurate in the smallest detail, of the Hagenbeck-Wallace Circus complete with circus wagons and rail cars. Here, as with the dollhouses, we see Alex's fascination with miniatures show itself again. Some behaviorists take a somewhat darker view and see fascination with miniatures as the need for control and dominance—standing above and manipulating. Perhaps Alex's desires were a good deal less sinister and just the continued collecting of a boy who never grew up and whose toy box was enormous indeed. He displayed the miniature circuses along a darkened and maze-like corridor and uncharacteristically made no changes or additions to the collection, as if lacking the energy to do so.

The Circus Miniatures

In the main Circus Building, a structure that is thirty-six-feet high, Alex conceived of a giant circus wagon and asked artist Terry English to come up with some conceptual designs, which he then used in the construction of the giant vehicle. An independent contractor and The House on the Rock staff built this wagon and an elephant pyramid reaching nearly to the ceiling. The centerpiece of the building is two conjoined elements: the Circus Wagon and the Circus Orchestra comprising 120 figures with animated musical instruments. The idea had its beginnings in the middle 1970s when Alex proposed an animated orchestra in conjunction with the organ in the original Organ Room. This would be his orchestrion *piece de resistance*, his grandest effort at extending the idea of a band organ outside of the box. It took years to lay the miles of wiring and air hoses, to build the pneumatics for the instrument animation, and equally as long to fashion the figures. It was time also for wily shop employees to fashion familiar portraits among the players, including a portrait of Alex himself. Although the room opened to the public in 1987, the Orchestra did not debut until May of 1990 (six months after Alex's death).

The Circus Orchestra

Around the outside walls of the Circus building he installed his collection of Baranger motions not just to look at but for the guests to operate. When it came to wheeling and dealing he still rose to the occasion. The Baranger motion collection was very appealing to Alex. In 1983 several hundred became available from California collector John Daniel. Between 1925 and 1959, the Baranger Company of South Pasadena manufactured small-animated tableaus that were rented to jewelry stores around the country on a rotating basis. The motions were placed in store windows as a point of interest and for diamond jewelry advertisement. When the company ceased business collector John Daniel ended up with a lot of the assets. By the 1980s Baranger motions were beginning to be noticed by collectors and the prices were going up. John Daniel heard that Alex had a collection of highly prized, hand-carved early twentieth-century carousel animals from the Dentzel Company. He had not used these very valuable figures on the grand carousel and decided to trade them to John for hundreds of Barangers.

The deal was completed over the phone as was common for Alex, and soon the truck from California along with two of John's employees arrived at The House on the Rock workshop. John Daniel flew in to join the trade. The Barangers were accounted for and the carousel animals were selected and loaded on the truck—oddly, Alex was not around. John and his helpers decided to go to lunch before leaving and in a little while Alex showed up at the shop and asked his employees to open up the truck. He looked at the animals that they had chosen and told his workers, "Unload these horses and I'll show you the ones to give them." The horses they had selected were outer row carousel horses that were more elaborately carved and hence more valuable—Alex had his staff replace them with inner row horses carved in a less detailed fashion and less valuable. A few days later, when the truck arrived back in California, Alex got a late-night call from South Pasadena. John and Alex conducted future trades and in the end both were satisfied: John expanded his carousel collection and Alex used the Baranger motions to fill the walls of the Circus Room.

Alex was always ready to respond to the unexpected, but never quite so much as when Jon Koss contacted him. Croatian by birth, during his career Jon toured the world of dance performance as a female impersonator. He had sewn all of his own costumes and now wanted to sell a large part of his wardrobe. Alex bought the whole thing and had them draped on mannequins posed on the elephant pyramid and the Circus Wagon, sequins and all.

The Elephant Pyramid

Great Circus Wagon

Whale Building, incomplete at the time of Alex's death, was at the center of his attention during the last years and months of his life. As a young man he built model ships, one of which he displayed in the original House before it was open to the public. His imagination was primed by the adventures of the sea depicted in the writing of Robert Louis Stephenson, Herman Melville, and Samuel Taylor Coleridge. The idea of The Whale Building gradually began to form in his mind in the early 1980s. He made a few entries in his notebooks and, as a starting point, had artist Terry English make some conceptual drawings of his ideas. In 1984 he commissioned The Stewart Johnson Design Studio in Milwaukee to build a scale model of a giant whale locked in combat with an enormous squid. He placed this model on display at The House on the Rock, advertising it as a future attraction. Meanwhile, he had Dave Nelson and his crew construct a huge building, six stories high and over 150-feet long, to house the whale and his growing collections of nautical artifacts.

He had collected the odd piece of memorabilia of the sea as he went along and eventually became fascinated with the art of scrimshaw (carvings and engravings done on bone or ivory). In the early 1980s Alex's principle finder was Tom Bradley who had been a driver for Tom Every and now, with Every gone, Bradley wandered far and near searching for artifacts to sell to Alex. He ran a small company in McFarland, Wisconsin whose chief business seems to have been finding and/or making artifacts for Alex. It was through Bradley that Alex acquired his enormous collection of reproduction and authentic scrimshaw as well as a host of other artifacts. Bradley's crew also custom-built model ships and other large models including a full-scale model of the nineteenth-century steam train "The General." Bradley had a very good run as Alex's finder but ran into various legal troubles and disappeared. His associate Steve Murray replaced him; Steve became a finder for Alex and along with his wife Elizabeth was energetic in searching out collectibles all over the world. In 1983 Alex sent them to the Mauritius Islands in the Indian Ocean to research the local model-ship-building industry. He ordered model ships through Steve from this source, many of which were used in The Whale Building. He commissioned local model makers to produce additional large models, some more than twenty feet in length. Once again the warehouses began to fill up with artifacts and models to be used in the new displays. The Museum of Ships and the Sea in Seattle became available and in 1987 Alex acquired the entire collection of ship models and historic artifacts.

The construction of the whale was an enormous undertaking in itself. He contracted Dave Oswald, who built fiberglass artifacts for Alex in the past. Dave completed large sections of the whale and began to assemble them in the new building, but he and Alex conflicted about procedures and money and were unable to come to an agreement about how to finish the project. Dave dropped out, but Alex continued on using The House on the Rock employees. Weak as he was, he surprised everybody, scaling the inside beams, and climbing to the top of the whale where he posed for what turned out to be a farewell photo in the mouth of the enormous sea creature.

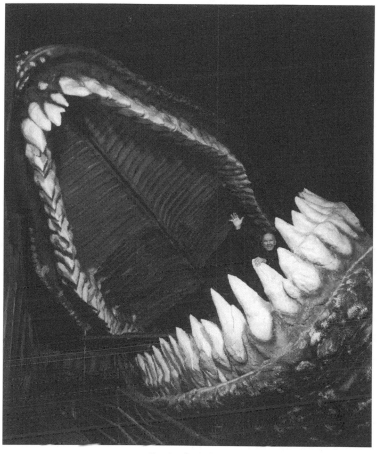

Alex in the Whale

Everything was in place for the completion of whale project when Alex died in November of 1989. Staff members finished The Whale Building after his death. Although Alex collected almost everything in the room and started the enormous project, there never were any plans and it cannot be said that the room is completely his design or that it would have been entirely pleasing to him. Although many decisions about design and scale were already made, the builders just continued on with what they had at hand, financed partly by the Jordan estate, and produced the exhibit in his memory. It is certainly probable that the inclusion of labels identifying historic artifacts from the Seattle museum would not have been his choice.

The Whale under construction

The third huge display that was underway at the end of Alex life was the Transportation Building (now known as The Tribute to Nostalgia). The enormous centerpiece Alex had conceived for the six-story building was to be an impossibly massive steam tractor towering to the ceiling. The actual plan and the building of this giant prop were left to Mike Olp, a woodworker from Brooklyn, Wisconsin. Mike had sold a few miniature wooden sleighs to Alex and came to visit Alex at the House. After touring the attraction for the first time, he recalled, "I was amazed and flabbergasted by all that I saw."[105]

Alex commissioned Mike to build a number of large royal coaches, steam locomotives, and other artifacts intended for the Transportation Building. They developed a close working relationship; Mike recalled, "He was a wonderful man. He'd come down to my shop on Fridays and look over what I'd done. I think he looked forward to it."[106] This glimpse into the gentler side of Alex is surprising to many who have dealt with him through the years and who thought of him as anything but avuncular. He visited Mike and his family every week, sitting in a chair much as he did in The House on the Rock workshops. Alex came to refer to him as "Sir Michael of Olp" and Mike named two of his children after Alex. The Transportation Building stood empty at the end of Alex's life and much of Mike's work went into storage.

Alex with custom carriage

In addition to the three huge projects Alex was moving forward on in his last years (The Whale Building, The Circus, and the Transportation Building), he also turned his attention to a number of collections he was gathering. These were installed in the section of The House on the Rock now referred to as The Galleries including: The Gun Collection, The Oriental Collection, The Armor Room, and The Crown Jewels.

From the very beginning Alex had a fascination with guns and his serious collecting began when in the 1960s he acquired many antique guns from the Ira Moody collection, most of which are on display in the Mill House. Along the way he picked up weapons that came up for sale. Now he put together a new collection of reproduction and fantasy weapons to be displayed in a new Gun Room. Mike Olp created individual wooden cases for this fantasy display of outlandish instruments of death and dismemberment. The old Alex touch rose here again as he designed a prosthetic leg with a derringer built into it, which Alex always claimed came from a Hayward, Wisconsin prostitute.

Prosthetic Leg

The Oriental Collection is an assemblage of ivories, ceramics, cork, and metal works collected from Asian suppliers. In 1986 Alex was careful to obtain a permit from the Fish and Wildlife Service, Division of Enforcement for the limited importation of ivory in compliance with national and international law. Here again, in spite of the fact that this is an extraordinary and authentic collection, the display is unadorned, although the artifacts are thoughtfully placed. It is also a study of how Alex could at one moment sink to the level of kitsch as has often been said of the flying semi-nude angels in the Carousel Room and in the next moment show a brilliant and exotic eye in the collection of Asian artifacts of beauty and skilled craftsmanship. On one hand he cared about what people thought and how it might affect business, while on the other hand he couldn't have cared less; he was really collecting and displaying at the end of his life to please himself and nobody else.

There was a slacking off here as the aging and tired Alex added nothing—he had no huge workshop project paralleling or enhancing the theme. He bought the objects and put them on display—as simple as that. He no longer could afford to expend a great deal of energy to manage large projects or to keep several balls in the air at once. There were just as many irons in the fire as there always were, but he was running out of energy. But there still was some gas in the tank.

The old ambitions to create overwhelming themed environments rose to the surface again in the Armor Room. Alex collected his first medieval armor reproduction in the mid 1960s when he purchased a few complete suits from Ira Moody. He picked up pieces as he went along but he always wanted a more complete display of reproductions. Alex commissioned armorer Terry English to come to The House on the Rock and create armor for him. Terry, who now lives in Cornwall, worked in The Tower of London collections and is the official armorer to Queen Elizabeth II. In addition, he is a well- respected designer and builder of historic and fantasy armor and costumes for Hollywood. His work has appeared in films such as *Dr. Zhivago, Excalibur, Aliens, Batman,* and *Harry Potter.* He was nominated for an academy award for his work on *Excalibur.* Terry set up in The House on the Rock workshops, and using ancient tools and techniques, created an array of armor for Alex.

The Armor Collection

Terry and Alex got along very well. Terry recalls, "Alex and I had so much in common, and we both knew we shared the same enthusiasm for creating wondrous things." Alex visited the workshop as he always had in the past and sat in his chair to watch Terry work. "I fondly remember Alex coming in to see what I was doing," Terry recalls, "sometimes he would sit in his chair and just look at what I was creating. I knew that deep down he just wanted to be doing it himself, but age had taken its toll."[107] They talked about a wide range of subjects as the work progressed. Terry created over sixty suits of armor for the display and for the massive battle scenes they were working on.

In a grand set, Alex had Terry create armor for a scene depicting Hannibal in the Second Punic War, during which he went into battle with armored elephants. The scene is a historical anachronism; while the elephant armor might be plausible for its time, the knights are from a time some hundreds of years later. This did not bother Alex. He was interested in the drama of the scene and did not trouble about the niceties of historical accuracy. And who could not be fascinated with the armored elephant and the giant armored dog? Terry recalls, "He told me that he was a showman, and his life was about entertaining the public." He also had Terry create a scene showing two Japanese mounted warriors in combat as well as two knights on horseback locked in battle.

Although the armor is well made and the general concept is imaginative and dramatic, the handling of the scenes is not up to the usual Jordan standards. He was tired and increasingly weaker; he simply did not have the energy he needed—this frustrated and saddened him. While Alex was running out of energy, Terry was running out of time and needed to move on. Terry looks back on these sets with mixed emotions and a bit of regret, wishing there had been more time to do the ideas justice. But he does carry with him good memories of his time with Alex, "We shared some imaginative ideas," he recalls, "it was almost as though we were one—our conversations were electrifying, to say the least."

This is one of the last grand schemes that Alex was able to finish, and while the concept and certainly the armor are inspired, it is easy to sense the struggle and impatience of a weakened man and a terrible loss of energy. Nonetheless, the giant dioramas scenes are witness to his determination to work to the end.

In his later years, Alex became something of an Anglophile, partly because of his lifelong reading of English history and his familiarity with English literature, but also because of his British friends Steve and Elizabeth Murray. They periodically returned to the UK on visits and found artifacts of interest for Alex. The Murrays along with Tom Bradley led Alex to a variety of collections of authentic artifacts as well as reproductions. He was fascinated by the heroics of Lord Nelson and had in mind a large animated scene of the Battle of Trafalgar for the Whale Room. When he read that the body of Admiral Nelson was preserved during its return to England in a barrel of brandy, he came up with the idea of having the Admiral bubble up out of a barrel in the corner of the room—an idea that did not see the light of day.

A collection of exact copies of the British crown jewels became available and he bought them, not because it made any sense, and he certainly wasn't trying to fool anybody—he just wanted them. They are displayed, museum style, at the end of the tour; he did not theme the area.

While the Galleries are not as compelling or dramatic as Alex's earlier work, they stand as a testament to his indomitable spirit and creativity in spite of his failing body.

Chapter 14

Selling the Dream

The first rumors that Alex was thinking about selling The House on the Rock surfaced in 1978 when he was in negotiations with Wisconsin Alumni Research Foundation (WARF), which is a well-endowed research institution connected to The University of Wisconsin; the House was then valued at somewhere between five and seven million. WARF sent members of their staff to The House on the Rock to look at the facility. As it turned out, The Foundation had real doubts about how they would be able to manage the complexities of the attraction, there was difficulty evaluating the assets, and they eventually backed away from consideration. Alex also had concerns about what his role would be after turning the attraction over to WARF; he was wary of bureaucracies, committees, and large organizations—the truth is that Alex was really not ready to make a deal with them or anybody else. He did, however express disappointment with the WARF trustees' decision not to purchase the attraction. They cited that they had no desire to move into new fields of endeavor. There were also tax problems for them; besides, their real mission was not running an attraction but supporting research.[108] They must also have realized what Alex was already aware of—the business was becoming complicated, difficult to manage, and, for Alex, an increasing burden. Alex was a hands-on owner/entrepreneur who was not about to cede control of any part of his business.

Alex hired John Korb as manager in the 1970s. He would remain on staff through the rest of Jordan's life, but Alex still controlled, as much as one could control such an amorphous enterprise, every detail of the business, a tiring task for a man in failing health who was now approaching his sixty-fifth birthday.

Korb managed as much as he was allowed. In 1978 Alex still had big plans for the future with the Carousel, the Organ Room, and further additions on the drawing boards, but he was still thinking about the future of The House on the Rock after his passing. There was a long-standing belief in the local community that Alex would end up leaving The House on the Rock to Iowa County and some long-term employees looked toward a future as government employees with benefits. In fact, a will drafted for Alex in 1970 named Iowa County as a beneficiary. Alex also made moves toward forming a foundation, even asking employees, the author among them, if they might be interested in being on the board. In 1979, still feeling positive, he told a *Wisconsin State Journal* reporter, "I want to finish my work out there and then I'll sell it. I'm only sixty-five years old and in good health. I've only got a couple of more years of work. I have to sell it sooner or later. You can't take it with you."[109]

A great deal of the management time was taken up in responding to constant requests from print publications and television for interviews and information about the attraction. Alex himself had stopped giving interviews in the 1960s, consenting only rarely to speak to the press. Hardly a week went by when there wasn't a media crew on the property; the task of handling all this fell to Korb, who became the spokesperson for The House on the Rock and stood between the media and his reclusive boss. As The House on the Rock became better known through national magazine articles and newspaper features as well as television productions, it was natural that Alex would attract the attention of those who were interested in owning the attraction. Oral history at The House on the Rock lists Marriot Corporation, actor Steve McQueen, Dolly Parton, and Hugh Hefner among those who expressed interest. Attorney John Mitby recalls, "He had a lot of candidates who had interest in it, groups from all across the United States. Alex wanted somebody with a business background because he was concerned the House wouldn't grow if it weren't economically viable. He didn't want somebody who would buy it and take all the money out of it."[110] What everyone involved understood was the present and future popularity of The House on the Rock. What they did not understand was that he was not yet ready to sell, and when he *was* ready to sell, *they* wouldn't stand a chance.

By 1986 things had changed, according to Attorney Mitby: "He never wanted to sell. The only time that changed was in the last three or four years of his life. He physically was not able to do the job he wanted to do on a day-by-day basis. His health was failing. Now he had something like a hundred employees. It was disappointing to him not to be able to be there day in and day out."[111]

The person who ended up owning The House on the Rock was Janesville businessman Art Donaldson. Art showed his determination to succeed even as a boy, mowing lawns, selling greeting cards and setting up lemonade stands. His entrepreneurial spirit was there from the beginning. The money he made was not for money's sake as he later recalled in what is his guiding principal: "You can't create things, build things, do things, unless you have money."[112]

Art grew up in Janesville, Wisconsin, and after high school and a stint in the army he came back home where he started a billboard and sign company along with his wife Karen. It was their hard work and persistence that led to success as he started to buy out his competitors. He is a man with the common touch, comfortable in casual clothes rather than a suit, whose word and handshake are his bond. He ran his company, Vivid, pretty much like Alex ran The House on the Rock, calling on his clients personally and keeping track of all the details of the business. When he went to Miller Brewing in Milwaukee to sell signs, he talked to Mr. Miller personally, so when he decided to call on The House on the Rock he wanted to talk directly with Mr. Jordan—not so easy.

Art's interest in tourism and attractions grew out of his outdoor advertising business, so it's no surprise he would eventually call on The House on the Rock. But there was something beyond business that attracted him. He knew from the first time he saw the attraction that it was a very special place, unlike anything he had ever seen. And that's saying something because Art, an intrepid traveler, had circled the globe several times. He wanted to meet Alex Jordan, the man behind this wild creativity.

He stopped by the House several times and asked to see Mr. Jordan. John Korb, ever protective of Alex's privacy, asked if he had an appointment and since he did not, Korb told him, "Mr. Jordan won't see you." When Art asked how he was ever going to meet this guy, Korb told him to call Alex at home at one or two in the morning and, "see if you can get an appointment." Reluctantly and incredulously, he called at 2 a.m. Not only did Alex answer—they talked for an hour and Art got his appointment.

Art Donaldson recalls: "After I talked to him, I found out that one of his real loves was signs. He didn't talk to hardly any sales people, but he'd talk to somebody who had some signs, I think I sold him some signs that first day." And that was the beginning of their friendship, as Art returned time after time to talk with Alex and to do a little business. Art remembers, "As the years went by, I developed as good a friendship as you could develop with Alex." Art was impressed by Alex's broad range of knowledge on a variety of subjects including business, commodities, current events, and said that Alex had the "best overall grasp of the total goings-on of business of anyone I've ever met."

Art and Alex had more in common than either of them thought. Art typifies a low-key upper Midwestern style—self effacing, casual in demeanor without a hint of slickness and ostentation, but underneath an industrious and informed businessman. Alex was never going to sell to anyone he was not comfortable with, and while offers and approaches by the rich and famous may have flattered him, they had no chance of being accepted. Out of the blue one day Alex said to Art, "You know, I'd sell this place."

Art responded, "Well, I'd sure like to figure out how I could buy it."

"Huum."

Ten or so years later, after a lot of visits, lots of billboards and late night phone calls, it was time—maybe. Attorney John Mitby reflected: "He [Alex] knew by then The House on the Rock was bigger than him or anybody else in the world. But he felt an obligation to the public to get somebody who would take care of it. He settled on Art. Art knew business, he knew attractions, and he had a family that could work with him." They had been talking casually back and forth for years about making a deal and in 1986 Art felt that it was time, and recalled, "I got indications that maybe he was serious." The two and a-half years that followed were filled with ups and downs as Alex asked Art to make a proposal, and Alex was not easily pinned down and was biding his time—time that was now precious for him. Finally all the accountants, attorneys, and other "suits" came up with a proposal. Jordan responded, "Well, yeah, maybe."

This was followed by a meeting of both sides, with number crunchers in three-piece suits sitting around a table thinking they had a deal. Everybody went home satisfied the deal was done. The next day Alex called to say, "The deal's off." It's likely that Alex was not comfortable with all these business types and bolted.

Art still visited Alex at home and finally, after more than two years, the time was right. Attorney Mitby told Art not to use any lawyers or accountants. Art went to Alex with a letter of intent and an offer and Alex said yes, but "First we have to go see Mitby." It was December of 1988 and Alex Jordan had eleven months to live. On the day of the sale Art showed up tired out—he and his wife Karen had been working hard on the deal and had been up through the previous night. Guess who showed up dressed in a suit coat and a tie, attorney and accountant in tow—Alexander John Jordan that's who. The old gray fox may have been tired, but he was in charge of the room and the deal. They all gathered around the table. Alex was generous and easy in the end, and they signed the deal for a reported $17.5 million and considerations and that was that.[113] The snapshot taken after the deal had been signed tells the whole story.

Alex Jordan with Art and Karen Donaldson at the sale of The House on the Rock

Art looks like he has just been put through an industrial washing machine, Alex is looming over the scene looking like he has just signed over his car to his son, and Karen looks like she's really happy that they can get their life back again. She is fond of recalling how Art related a story of Alex's attempt at fishing (see Chapter 2) in which Alex claims to be no fisherman. She said, "Oh yes, he's a fisherman—he's been playing with you and reeling you in for years." Art was aware that if Alex had shopped The House on the Rock around he could have gotten much more for it. After the sale Alex turned to Art and said, "Remember, you're an entertainer."

Alex was now the Creative Director of The House on the Rock with a salary of $500,000 per year. He did not live long enough to collect the full first year. He returned most of his salary into the projects he was working on even though he no longer owned the attraction. Art and Alex collaborated during the time remaining. Art recalls, "He didn't interfere. Which I give him a lot of credit for. There had to be a few things that bothered him...we became closer over the time we worked together. I just wish it could have been longer. In a way, he became almost a dad in the way he treated me. Maybe he didn't always like what I did, but he was very supportive."

CHAPTER 15
THE DEATH OF ALEX JORDAN

In the last year of his life Alex slowly faded, finding it hard to drive out to The House on the Rock and cutting his visits down to three or four per week. He sometimes showed up uncharacteristically wearing a hat like the retired guests who came through the attraction. He was still burning with ideas and did the best he could to keep track of the major projects underway. He was weaker and could walk only short distances and often returned home exhausted. But he would continue to the end still interested even "at the close of day."

He visited his cardiologist more frequently as his heart condition worsened through the year. Doctors had been advising bypass surgery for a number of years but Alex always refused; he was not eligible for a heart transplant because of his condition and age. In October 1989 he was admitted to intensive care at Meriter-Methodist Hospital in Madison. Nobody seemed to be accepting the end was near except Alex, who asked to be removed from intensive care when he understood the prognosis. Jennie visited, as did Julie Esser and a number of employees, including the team working on the Whale Room with whom he talked about the Packers and how he wanted to get back out to The House on the Rock. Art Donaldson visited and found Alex's mind sharp; they conversed as he drifted in and out, taking up the conversation where they had left off. When Art was getting ready to leave he said, "You have to get well, Alex, so you can get out there and get to those projects."

Alex responded, "You've got good people out there. Don't worry, you don't need me."[114]

Jennie was there at the end and later in the day employees at The House on the Rock were called and told that if they wanted to see Alex they should come. Many came and saw him for one last time. Neil Hanson recalled that in the end Alex became, "a nice older guy who had his extended family out here [at the House] and he enjoyed it." On that day, November 6, they were gathered there and as Neil recalled, "His heart was failing. You could see it on the monitor. But I was struck by how aware he was. A new person would come in and he'd ask how they were doing. Then he'd drift off." Later that afternoon, surrounded by friends and members of his employee family, Alex died. He was seventy-five.

He was larger than life to those who worked for him and he filled the room he entered. There was that sense that something might happen— something good, something not so good, but things were not going to be the same when he was around. Sycophants, admirers, surrounded him as well as the level headed who viewed him with varying degrees of respect and sometimes admiration. He had his share of detractors who wanted him to be somebody else. He never tried to be anybody else, never pretended or put on airs—he was just himself. He gave not a damn about what people thought of him or said about him, correcting neither false accusations, nor exaggerated claims made on his behalf. Alex was not some dreamy artist who lived in a precious fantasy world; he was down-to-earth and smart with an eye not only for the created objects that would advance his vision and his business, but also with a sixth sense that enabled him to recognize, and retain for a time, the talented people who could work with him to achieve his vision. He could be generous and stingy, kindly and mean, brilliant and dense, willful, lazy, industrious, cultured, common. Nobody can deny he left behind a unique and fascinating legacy. There was a fire burning there—it warmed some and it singed others. He seemed to have no regrets. He was comfortable in his own skin.

Now came forward a man from Milwaukee claiming to be Alex's son. There were always rumors that Alex had fathered a son. Alex's attorney, John Mitby, made sure that the process of carrying out Alex's will allowed time for DNA samples to be taken from Alex's remains and sent to a lab to be compared with the claimant. The results showed that the claimant could not be Alex's son. Attorney Mitby summed it up, "At this point in time, although this person may well believe that he had some relationship with Alex

Jordan, the scientific evidence and other evidence does not support such a claim."[115] The court agreed. Attorney Mitby and the claimant's attorney came to a nominal settlement and the claim was withdrawn. Corollary to this, a suggestion that Alex had been married in 1933 and divorced three years later was not supported by any state records.

Soon all the loose ends were tied up and all of the resources (including Alex's home in Madison) were gathered together, along with $100,000 cash Alex had stashed under his bed—a child of the Depression to the end. Most of his estate was left to Jennie Olson, his companion for over fifty years. In the final days of Alex's life there was talk of the two of them marrying, but nothing ever came of it. As a result the Federal Government took a sizeable chunk of the estate in taxes. He bequeathed amounts ranging from $50,000 to $250,000 tax-free to more than a dozen individuals, many of whom were employees.

Alex Jordan's remains were cremated and scattered from a low-flying airplane as it circled the House, returning what was left of Alex Jordan to the place that he said was "Everything I ever loved."

Jennie Olson continued her simple ways, living in the same apartment where she had lived with Alex, missing him, and fondly remembering their years together. She died in 2006 at age ninety-five, leaving behind several bequests and The Jennie H. Olson Charitable Foundation.

As for Alex, he remains at The House on the Rock: "Present, but not voting."

Portrait of Alex Jordan (early 1970s)

Afterword

W hen Alex passed away he left behind him a sprawling, popular attraction that during the season employed over one hundred people and an owner who now had to move forward without his visionary guidance.

The creative life is always an unfinished life, and the clear-headed Alex had ideas and projects to the end. He always preferred the company and energy of people younger than himself; he left behind a staff at the height of their abilities, but there was much work to be done. The large projects remaining were The Whale Building, the Transportation Building, the nearly finished Circus Orchestra, and the Blue Danube music machine. As owner Art Donaldson put it, "Alex had several years of planning and construction underway at the time of his death...it's going to take a number of years."[116]

And Art had ideas of his own. While he had great respect for and even awe at the creative work of Alex Jordan, there were areas in which he wanted to bring *his* vision and abilities to bear—marketing, promotion, and customer services. He summed it up: "My role here will be devoted mostly to promotion and improving the amenities of the place to best serve the people. We will be doing more joint marketing with other tourist attractions to get our message out in the state and surrounding states." In addition to tackling the creative projects then underway he initiated one of his own, The Alex Jordan Creative Center.

Shortly after Alex's death in the fall of 1989, work began in a full frontal assault on all of these projects. Everything, with the exception of The Alex Jordan Creative Center, was in process by then, but now the work was infused with a new energy.

The Whale Building project had slowed down to a near stop towards the end of Alex's life and in September 1989 was put on temporary hold while Alex directed the installation of a small Japanese Garden adjacent to The Moongate.

This was the last project completed under Alex's direction at The House on the Rock. As winter approached work on the Whale Room resumed under the direction of the author, in the company of Steve Schaaf and Clark Mindermann who had worked with Alex on the room.

The Whale Room (now renamed The Heritage of the Sea) opened in May 1990. The Blue Danube music machine, which had been in development for fifteen years, fell to Neil Hanson, music machine technician and, in the Alex era, member of the board of The House on the Rock. Neil recalled, "It was unnerving in a way. The Blue Danube was visually intact—Alex had done that. We knew he wanted the 'Blue Danube Waltz' to play. But Alex always made the artistic decisions so you always knew exactly how something should look and function. It was hard. I think we got close to what he wanted, but you don't know. I'm sure he would have had an extra touch or two."

Construction of The Alex Jordan Creative Center at The House on the Rock workshops was completed in the winter of 1989–1990. When the Center opened it provided guided tours of the workshops tracing, the history of Alex's life and The House on the Rock through a behind-the-scenes look at the place where much of the production took place.

The House on the Rock expanded its season in 1991, opening a Christmas tour featuring a collection of over 6,000 Santas gathered over years by Art's wife Karen. The company continued to improve guest services with the addition of new restrooms, restaurant facilities, and heating and air conditioning. In late 1989 Art's daughter Sue began working at The House on the Rock, bringing her education (Masters Degree in Business) and skills to the management side of the attraction. By 1992 she was familiar enough with The House on the Rock to be appointed President. The House on the Rock expanded into the hotel business in 1998 with the opening of The House on the Rock Inn located in Dodgeville, Wisconsin. In 1999 Art purchased The Springs Resort and Golf Course seven miles north, renaming it The House on the Rock Resort thereby adding 80 additional hotel rooms, a golf course, and other resort amenities to The House on the Rock business. Alex wanted to sell to someone who was not going to sit on his hands and let The House on the Rock slide into decline or sell the place off piece by piece, but he could never have dreamed how much expansion there would be.

The House on the Rock continued to renew and broaden its operations in the new millennium with the 2003 purchase of another hotel in Dodgeville and the 2005 remodeling of an existing restaurant at the attraction. A major remodeling of the attraction began in 2008 with the building of a new Welcome Center and a Japanese Garden. In 2010 the attraction opened The Alex Jordan Center, which houses a collection of artifacts and information about the life and work of Alex Jordan.

Through all of this The House on the Rock continues to draw thousands of visitors from around the world, and its appeal has broadened to include new generations who marvel at the wonders Alex Jordan created on a rock and on the surrounding hillsides in southwestern Wisconsin.

Don Martin, who built so much of it with Alex, summed it up: "It's remarkable…a little place like this, hidden in the woods, to have become so popular."

The House on the Rock

Endnotes

Chapter 1

1. Emma Lazarus (1849–87), from the inscription on the pedestal of the Statue of Liberty.

2. Information about the families and details about their immigration are taken from, *Swiss Roots: Seiler Genealogy and History*, 1290–1980, Editor/Author, Mary Esther Wolf-Riedy M.S. pp18ff.

3. *The Wisconsin State Journal*, 11/09/13. p5.

4. The Greenbush neighborhood deteriorated over the years and became recognized as sub standard housing, and as the twentieth century neared its mid point it was sometimes referred to as a slum. In the 1960s, as part of the nationwide urban renewal program, nearly the entire neighborhood was demolished and replaced with apartments, a medical center, etc.

Chapter 2

5. *Alex Jordan: Architect of His Own Dream*, by Doug Moe, 1990, The House on the Rock, p16.

6. *Knight Life*, October, 1987, by Linda Tutt.

7. From the transcript of an interview conducted by the author with Tom Every in 2010.

8. Jennie related this story to her nephew, James Eisele, who told it to the author in an interview in 2013.

9. Moe, p72.

10. From Eisele interview.

11. From written transcripts of recorded interviews conducted by Doug Moe in 1990.

12. *The Uplands Reader II*, 1981, Edna Meudt, ed.

CHAPTER 3

13.   William Wordsworth, "Lines composed a Few Miles above Tintern Abbey, " in *The Essential Wordsworth*, Galahad Books, New York, 1993 Seamus Heaney ed. p. 44.

14.   Meudt, op.cit.

15.   Series of articles by Marv Balousek, *The Wisconsin State Journal*, that later were compiled into a self-published book.

16.   From the Doug Moe transcript of an interview conducted by John Korb and Neil Hanson on March 2, 1990.

17.   More information about Sid Boyum @ www.designcoalition.org.

18.   From a 1971 extended interview with Kimberly Clark.

19.   Ibid.

20.   *The Milwaukee Journal*, 11/8/59.

21.   From a 2013 interview with Nancy Schaaf; Jennie related this to her after Alex's death.

22.   This model is now on display in the Alex Jordan Center at The House on the Rock.

23.   Moe, p58.

24.   Martin quotes Moe, p40ff.

25.   *The Milwaukee Journal*, 3/23/72, by Steve Hannah.

26.   *The Wisconsin State Journal*, 9/2/70, by Barbara Reinherz.

27.   *The Milwaukee Journal*, 11/8/59.

28.   *The Milwaukee Journal*, 11/8/59.

29.   The Way of the Cross, also called The Stations of the Cross, is a Catholic practice which involves twelve relief sculptures (sometimes paintings) depicting the events of Good Friday. The faithful move from one station to another meditating on the scenes.

30.   More information about the building and significance of The Infinity Room in Chapter 12.

31.   Moe transcripts.

32.   Moe, p83.

33. More information about Bob Searles in Chapter 7.

34. *The Capital Times*, 8/6/62, August Derleth.

35. Moe, p44.

36. Kimberley Clark interview 1971.

37. Quotes from Lynn and Homer Fieldhouse are from Moe p51.

38. More information about Don Blanding and *Vagabond's House* at donblanding.com.

CHAPTER 4

39. The author never saw these works in place but has studied the Room and come to this conclusion—visit and judge for yourself.

40. Biographical information from, *A Basket of Sculptured Thoughts*, by Gladys Llewellyn Walsh (self published) Straus Printing Co., Madison, Wisconsin.

41. Moe 68.

42. From a press release written for The House on the Rock dated 4/25/64.

43. Taken from Moe, p73–4.

44. Mobile phones were almost unheard of in those days.

45. *The Wisconsin State Journal* 9/2/70, Barbara Reinherz.

CHAPTER 5

46. Moe, p13.

47. As told to the author by Steve Schaaf in 2013.

CHAPTER 6

48. Information about and quotes from Paul Yank are taken from Doug Moe interview notes.

49. From a note written by Bob Searles to the author, 4/18/10.

50. Information about Bob Searles is taken from his own documents donated to The House on the Rock archives in 2010.

51.   See Chapter 13 for more information about Art Donaldson and the sale.

52.   Gabler, Neal, *Walt Disney: The Triumph of The American Imagination*, Vintage Books, a Division of Random House Inc., New York. 2007, pp 498-9.

53.   Ibid. p161.

54.   Greg Burk quotes from Doug Moe interview transcripts.

55.   *The Milwaukee Journal*, 3/23/75, by Steve Hannah.

56.   Eisele interview 2013.

57.   Moe, p103.

CHAPTER 7

58.   Moe, p8.

59.   Moe transcripts

60.   Quotes from Jim McKahan from an interview with the author in 2010.

61.   In *Pride and Prejudice*, by Jane Austen.

62.   From the transcript of an interview with Doug Moe.

63.   A will dated 1970 did make this provision that was removed from later wills in the 80s.

64.   Moe, p43.

65.   From documents in The House on the Rock archives.

66.   Information about the investigation is from an e-mail to the author (10/17/13) from Q. David Bowers who was then a dealer in antique music machines and who was visited by the representatives of the Attorney General in 1978.

67.   *The Capital Times* 10/11/78.

68.   Ibid.

CHAPTER 8

69.   As told to the author in 2013 by the employee referred to here, Tom Kenyon.

70.   Moe, p37.

71. Ibid.

72. More information in Chapter 7.

73. From a 1990 tour script by Neil Hanson.

74. In a conversation with the author on the author's second day of employment.

Chapter 9

75. From the transcript of interview 1/14/12 at his residence.

76. Ibid.

77. Ibid.

78. Additional information about Tom Every (Dr. Evermor) in the author's book: *A Mythical Obsession*, Chicago Review Press, 2008.

79. Later, when Alex and Tom were at loggerheads Alex would claim that there was no such agreement. Eventually the case was settled out of court Alex claiming there had been no agreement (there was never anything in writing) but issuing a settlement check to Tom for $25,000.

80. Further information about Alex Jordan's Circus interests in Chapter 12.

81. *The Milwaukee Journal* 3/23/75, by Steve Hannah.

82. *Damn Good Advice*, by George Lois, Phaidon Press, New York, 2012.

83. For more information about Tom Every (Dr. Evermor) and his relationship with Alex Jordan see the author's biography of Tom, *A Mythic Obsession*, Chicago Review Press, 2008.

84. *The Catholic Imagination*, Andrew Greeley, University of California Press, Berkeley, LA, London, 2000 p.1.

Chapter 10

85. For a wider treatment of Cabinets of Curiosities see *Cabinets of Curiosities* by Patrick Mauries in the bibliography.

86. *Cabinets of Curiosities* by Patrick Mauries, Thames and Hudson 2011, p67.

87. Quotes from P.T. Barnum from: *P. T. Barnum: America's Greatest Showman*, Philip B. Kunhardt, Jr., Philip B Kunhardt III, and Peter W. Kundhardt, Alfred A. Knopf, 1995. pp. 136–141.

88.   Ibid.

89.   From *The Nation* July 27, 1865 at the web address: chnm, gmu, edu/lostmuseum/lm/276/.

90.   Although the "sucker born every minute" statement is often attributed to Barnum, scholars have searched high and low and have been unable to find that he ever said it. Those who knew him also deny the statement. He did say, "There's a customer born every minute."

91.   Information about The Museum of Jurassic Technology is from *Mr. Wilson's Cabinet of Wonder*, by Lawrence Weschler, Random House, New York, 1995.

CHAPTER 11

92.   *Collecting: An Unruly Passion*, Werner Muesterberger, Harcourt and Brace Company, New York, 1994, (and quoting Walter Benjamin in note p257), p24.

93.   Ibid. p31.

94.   Ibid. p135.

95.   Ibid. p254.

96.   See Chapter 2 for the remarks of Sid Boyum.

97.   Information about this affair was related to the author by Harry Hitchner in the late 1970s.

98.   For years the oral tradition at The House on the Rock was that Alex died at 4:15—the death certificate says 4:32. The clock had previously been set to the old time—the author set it to the correct time in 2013.

99.   In the darker times to follow the plaque was removed.

100. Jane Smiley, *Wisconsin: Three Visions Attained*, *The New York Times* 3/7/93.

101. As told to the author by Ron Boley in 2013.

CHAPTER 12

102. An undated quote from an in-house House on the Rock Publication.

103. Information about the design and construction process is taken from the transcript of a video produced about the project in the early 90s.

CHAPTER 13

104. "Do Not Go Gentle Into That Good Night" by Dylan Thomas, in *The Mentor Book of Major British Poets*, p553f.

105. Moe, p118.

106. Ibid. p118.

107. Quotes from Terry English are from an e-mail from Terry to the author in 2013.

CHAPTER 14

108. Information taken from a letter in The House on the Rock Archives from Attorney John Mitby to Alex Jordan, 10/24/79.

109. *The Wisconsin State Journal*, 5/23/79.

110. Moe, p122.

111. Ibid.

112. The Art Donaldson and Alex Jordan quotes that follow are from Moe, p97ff.

113. The suit coat was the same one he purchased at Brooks Brothers in New York City more than twenty years before—although the fit by now was somewhat less tailored.

CHAPTER 15

114. Quotes here from Moe, p128f.

115. *The Wisconsin State Journal*, 5/18/90.

AFTERWORD

116. Quotes here from Moe, p131ff.

Bibliography

Buck, Patricia Ringling, *The John and Mable Ringling Museum of Art*, Santa Barbara, California, Albion Publishing Company, 1988.

Gabler, Neal, *Walt Disney: The Triumph of The American Imagination*, New York, Random House, 2006.

Goodwin, Joscelyn, *Athanasius Kircher's Theater of the World*, Rochester, Vermont, Inner Traditions, 2009.

Greeley, Andrew, *The Catholic Imagination*, Los Angeles and Berkeley, University of California Press, 2000.

Harris, Neil, *Humbug: The Art of P.T. Barnum*, Chicago, University of Chicago Press, 1973.

Kunhardt, Phillp B. Jr., Kunhardt, Philip B. III, and Kunhardt, Petcr W., *P.T. Burnum: America's Greatest Showman*, New York, Alfred A. Knopf, 1995.

Kupsh, Tom, *A Mythic Obsession: The World of Dr. Evermor*, Chicago, Chicago Review Press, 2008.

Levitan, Stuart D., *Madison. The Illustrated Sesquicentennial History, Volume I, 1856-1931*, Madison, The University of Wisconsin Press, 2006.

Lois, George, *Damn Good Advice*, New York, Phaidon Press, 2012.

Mauries, Patrick, *Cabinets of Curiosities*, London, Thames and Hudson, 2002.

Merritt, Christopher, and Lynxwiler, J. Eric, *Knott's Preserved*, Santa Monica, California, Angel City Press, 2010.

Moe, Doug, *Alex Jordan: Architect of His Own Dream*, Spring Green, Wisconsin, The House on the Rock, 1990.

Muensterberger, Werner, *Collecting: An Unruly Passion*, New York, Harcourt Brace, 1994.

Weschler, Lawrence, *Mr. Wilson's Cabinet of Wonder*, New York, Random House, 1995.

Index

Made in the USA
Lexington, KY
21 October 2017